28\9

Self-Esteem and Body Image

Independence

Educational Publishers

Cambridge

First published by Independence
PO Box 295
Cambridge CB1 3XP
England

British Library Cataloguing in Publication Data
Self-Esteem and Body Image – (Issues Series)
I. Donnellan, Craig II. Series
158.1

ISBN 1 86168 350 2

Printed in Great Britain
MWL Print Group Ltd

Layout by
Lisa Firth

Cover
The illustration on the front cover is by
Simon Kneebone.

CONTENTS

Chapter One: Self-Esteem – The Facts

Chapter Two: Self-Esteem and Body Image

Chapter Three: Raising Self-Esteem

Introduction

Self-Esteem and Body Image is the one hundred and seventeenth volume in the **Issues** series. The aim of this series is to offer up-to-date information about important issues in our world.

Self-Esteem and Body Image looks at the facts of self-esteem, the relationship between self-esteem and body image and the issue of raising low self-esteem.

The information comes from a wide variety of sources and includes:
Government reports and statistics
Newspaper reports and features
Magazine articles and surveys
Website material
Literature from lobby groups
and charitable organisations.

It is hoped that, as you read about the many aspects of the issues explored in this book, you will critically evaluate the information presented. It is important that you decide whether you are being presented with facts or opinions. Does the writer give a biased or an unbiased report? If an opinion is being expressed, do you agree with the writer?

Self-Esteem and Body Image offers a useful starting-point for those who need convenient access to information about the many issues involved. However, it is only a starting-point. Following each article is a URL to the relevant organisation's website, which you may wish to visit for further information.

*****

Self-esteem

Information from NetDoctor

What is self-esteem?

We all use the expression 'self-esteem', but what do we mean by it?

Some people think that self-esteem means confidence – and of course confidence comes into it – but it's rather more than that.

The fact is that there are any number of apparently confident people who can do marvellous things but who have poor self-esteem. Many people in the public eye fall into this category. Actors and comedians and singers in particular can seem to glow with assurance 'on stage', and yet off-stage many of them feel desperately insecure.

Indeed, individuals can be stunningly attractive and world-famous, and seem poised and perfect – yet still, deep down, find it hard to value themselves. Think of the late Princess of Wales and Marilyn Monroe and you'll accept, I think, that public adulation is no guarantee of self-belief.

By Christine Webber,
Psychotherapist and
Lifecoach

So, if self-esteem isn't quite the same thing as confidence, what is it?

Well, the word 'esteem' comes from a Latin word which means 'to estimate'. So, self-esteem is how you estimate yourself.

To do that you need to ask yourself certain questions:

- Do I like myself?
- Do I think I'm a good human being?
- Am I someone deserving of love?
- Do I deserve happiness?
- Do I really feel – both in my mind and deep in my guts – that I'm an OK person?

People with low self-esteem find it hard to answer 'yes' to these questions. Perhaps you are one of them. If so, what can you do?

How can you improve your self-esteem?

You can begin by accepting that you are certainly not alone. Masses of people have this problem.

Secondly, you can take on board a very important fact, which is that you are a wonderful, individual and special person – and there is no one quite like you. Your fingerprints and your DNA are totally different from everybody else's – unless you happen to have an identical twin. And your mind – and how it thinks and operates – is absolutely your own. This means that out of six billion people in the world, you are a one-off. So if nature has bothered to make you utterly unique, don't you feel that you should accept that you're important, and that you have as much right as anyone else to be on this planet?

You have other rights too. One of them is the right to make mistakes. Don't forget that 'to err is human' and most of us do much of our learning through getting things wrong before we get them right.

Furthermore, we have the right to respect ourselves – and to be respected: this is very important. And finally – and perhaps most vitally of all – we have the right to say 'yes' or 'no' for ourselves.

Many people with poor self-esteem think that they're not very important and that their views carry no weight. Is this you? If so, try to stop these destructive thoughts; because if you go around believing them, you'll encourage other people to believe them too.

Instead, start thinking of yourself – with your individual DNA, fingerprints and mind – as someone who has rights and opinions and ideas that are just as valid as anyone else's. This will help you to improve your 'self-estimation'.

Techniques to improve self-esteem

10-minute technique

People with poor self-esteem often fail to give themselves enough time and space. So find 10 minutes every day to be alone and to just sit and do nothing. Some people find it helpful to close their eyes and imagine a country scene or the sight and sound of waves gently lapping against the seashore. During this 10 minutes, allow yourself to feel peaceful and happy. Enjoy this time. It is yours – and yours alone. And you deserve it.

Finding 10 minutes for you is a caring thing to do and you will feel better for doing it.

Accentuate the positive

Often we make ourselves unhappy because we go over and over mistakes that we have made. But we can feel happier, and improve our self-esteem, if we rethink those things we believe we have done wrong or badly.

For example, one of my clients has to give presentations at work. He used to mentally beat himself up after every one. He would go over and over tiny errors in his mind. Now he writes an account of each presentation shortly after he's given it. And I have encouraged him to write about all the things that went well – not badly. He doesn't need to write about the bad things – they will stick in his memory and he will try hard not to repeat them. But he will forget the good things – unless he writes them down.

So when you have a bad day, or something goes wrong in your relationship or at work, write an account of what went right with that episode, not what went wrong. The results will surprise you – and improve how you see yourself.

List 50 things you like about yourself

If you're seriously lacking in self-esteem this could take weeks! But persevere.

You can write down your characteristics, or things about your looks. You can even write down things that you do that you happen to like about yourself. For example, you may buy a copy of *The Big Issue* on a day when you're feeling particularly short of money

> *When you have a bad day, or something goes wrong in your relationship or at work, write an account of what went right with that episode, not what went wrong*

yourself, or you may help an elderly woman in the supermarket sort out how much her groceries are going to cost, even though you're rushing to get your own shopping done in your lunch hour.

When you have reached your 50 good things, keep the list somewhere you can see it all the time.

Next comes an even harder part. Try to record one more, new thing you like about yourself every day for the rest of your life!

Getting and giving criticism

One of the areas that people with low self-esteem have greatest difficulty with is criticism – giving as well as receiving it. Both can be extraordinarily difficult. In fact some individuals are absolutely demolished by criticism, but it's something we cannot avoid.

Now, criticism is often unfair – and when it is we need to counter it by putting our own case succinctly and calmly. But some criticism is justified – and when we're sensible we can learn from it.

Often when we're criticised, we're so hurt that we start excusing ourselves and rebutting what's being said without really listening to it.

A mature, self-possessed person listens to criticism without interrupting. If there are aspects to the criticism that are valid, s/he begins by agreeing with those points. If s/he's unsure what's being said, s/he asks for clarification. If indeed s/he realises s/he was wrong, s/he says so and apologises. But if s/he disagrees with the criticism, s/he smiles and says: 'I'm afraid I don't agree with you.'

Now, it takes quite a lot of practice to feel and act this cool. So let's go through it again. When someone criticises you:

- listen – don't interrupt or start excusing yourself
- agree – where possible
- ask for clarification
- when you're wrong, admit it and apologise
- if criticism is wrong or unfair say: 'I'm afraid that I don't agree with you.'

Now, let's look at giving criticism, because people with poor-self-esteem often find it harder to dish out criticism than receive it. In fact many adults actually avoid promotion because they can't face the prospect of being in authority and having to criticise others.

So, how can you learn to criticise when you have to?

First of all, keep calm. Secondly, try to make your criticism at an

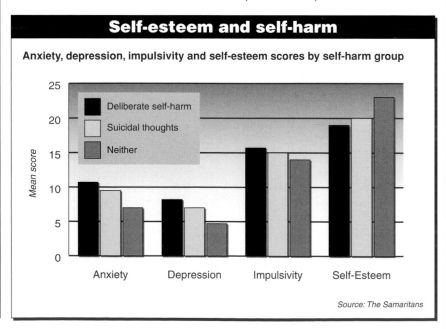

Self-esteem and self-harm

Anxiety, depression, impulsivity and self-esteem scores by self-harm group

- Deliberate self-harm
- Suicidal thoughts
- Neither

Mean score (y-axis: 0, 5, 10, 15, 20, 25)

(x-axis categories: Anxiety, Depression, Impulsivity, Self-Esteem)

Source: The Samaritans

appropriate time, rather than waiting till you're so fed up that you're furiously angry – when you'll be bound to make a mess of it.

Often we make ourselves unhappy because we go over and over mistakes that we have made

---

Take some deep breaths when you know you've got to criticise someone. Then try a technique called the 'criticism sandwich'. This means that you say something nice to the person you're criticising, then you insert the criticism, then you end with something else nice or positive or flattering. So, you might say to your secretary for example: 'Suzie, your work is usually absolutely great. But it's not quite right today and I'm afraid I'll have to ask you to re-do that report. I know it's most unlike you to get things wrong, you're so dependable and I want you to know how much I value you.'

You might notice that people who are good and fair when they criticise, tend to use the word 'I' rather than the word 'you'. This is because the word 'I' shows you're in control and that you've thought about what you're saying. All too frequently when we're out of control we don't say anything initially, which is when

we should address the problem. Instead we bottle it up till we explode. Then we use the words 'you', 'you're' and 'your' all the time. We say: 'You're bloody lazy.' Or 'You've got a down on me.' Or 'You make me sick.' These kinds of phrases sound very angry and accusatory. They also show that we're not in control. And after uttering them we generally feel worse about ourselves and our self-esteem plummets even more.

So just to recap, when criticising:

■ use the word 'I', not the word 'you'
■ keep calm and do some deep breathing
■ use the 'criticism sandwich' technique
■ also always try to criticise a person's behaviour rather than the person.

These tips are just as handy when it comes to standing up for yourself in other situations. And they're very useful when you want to be able to say 'no' without feeling guilty. Just keep calm and use the word 'I'.

Say: 'I won't be coming to that party with you.' Or: 'I'm afraid I won't be making tea at the cricket club on Saturday as I want to go shopping.' Or: 'I can't work late tonight, I'm sorry. But if necessary I'll happily stay tomorrow.'

People with poor self-esteem are always getting talked into doing things that they don't want to do. Does this sound like you? If so, it

must stop if you want to value yourself more. So learning how to stay calm and just say 'no' is very important.

Further help
Assertiveness classes
In the UK there are assertiveness classes throughout the country. This is further proof – if any were needed – that many people feel they are lacking in self-esteem. To find out what's available in your area, ask at your local public library. They usually have details of all types of evening classes and further education classes including those in assertiveness. Failing that, your local Citizens' Advice Bureau may be able to help. Or the Further Education department of your local council should be able to give you information.

If you learn to be more assertive, you may still need some work or some help on feeling better about yourself, but at least you'll have learned how to present yourself better – and that in itself will improve your self-regard.

Useful books
There are many books that can help you with issues of poor self-esteem. Here are just a few of them:
■ *The confidence to be yourself* by Dr Brian Roet, published by Piatkus.
■ *Overcoming low self-esteem* by Melanie Fennell, published by Robinson.
■ *Get the self-esteem habit* by Christine Webber, published by Hodder.
■ *Mind Over Mood* by Greenberger and Padesky, published by Guilford Press.
■ *Life coaching – change your life in 7 days* by Eileen Mulligan, published by Piatkus.
■ *Confidence works* by Gladeana McMahon, published by Sheldon.
■ *Life coaching – a cognitive-behavioural approach* by Michael Neenan and Windy Dryden, published by Brunner-Routledge.

■ The above information is re-printed with kind permission from NetDoctor. Visit www.netdoctor. co.uk for more information.

© NetDoctor

Background to self-esteem and how it can evolve

Information from Shining Bright

At any age, we seek encouragement and approval. This manifests itself from infancy and as we grow older, we begin to realise that today's society and culture does not readily address this. We receive constant messages from television, magazines, our place of work etc. that we should be attractive, slim, successful, fashionable, rich, have a large house and so on. The list is endless.

It is difficult for us to reach a level of balance as to who we are against our peers and how much self-belief and pride we should demonstrate. This can easily be perceived as arrogance or conceit instead of a healthy acknowledgement of our abilities and achievements. Success is however a great boost to the ego, yet we are influenced not just by our own levels of attainment but also the levels achieved by those people that we share relationships with or whose opinions we value and respect.

> *It is difficult for us to reach a level of balance as to who we are against our peers and how much self-belief and pride we should demonstrate*

For example, we tend to seek feedback from those whose opinions matter to us and whom we value. If those people have a low opinion of us or are negative in their responses, this can feel like a dent to our self-esteem. The other aspect to consider is that there are a group of people whose opinions matter to us due to the role they play in our lives, such as parents, teachers and bosses for example. As we often interact with them on a frequent basis, this can be an important source of feedback on our performance and behaviour. It is not necessary to like the people who play these roles in our lives, but their opinions matter to us nonetheless and influence our self-esteem.

We would all like to be able to add value, to contribute, to be included – in short, to matter. There are many factors in our lives which can contribute to low self-esteem which is why this is something which can fluctuate, depending on events and circumstances. Measuring ourselves against others can be a positive process, which allows us to learn and appreciate. It can also have a very negative impact, resulting in feeling inadequate or insecure. This 'self-judgement' or the perceived judgement of others can impact our ability to view ourselves objectively and achieve our dreams.

Power

Much of our self-esteem is based on the idea of 'power'. People with low self-esteem believe that any successes they achieve are attributable to luck rather than ability or competence. Equally, anything negative can be put down to factors beyond their control. Indeed, studies have shown that having choices in life can be significant in dictating levels of self-esteem. People who find themselves in a genuine or perceived position of powerlessness can suffer from stress and low self-esteem as they feel unable to control aspects of their lives or a particular situation.

People who have healthy self-esteem tend to attribute achievements and successes to qualities that they possess and the effective use of them. This generates a feeling of power and self-worth.

Communication

For those suffering with low self-esteem, social situations can present further difficulties and stress. They will most likely appear to lack confidence or may overcompensate and appear to be arrogant or overbearing. This comes from the need to seek approval from those in our social or peer groups and the result can be hesitant speech punctuated by unconvincing opinions or thoughts. Those with healthy self-esteem, by comparison, are able to appear confident with strong self-belief and opinions. They are also able to take a risk during a conversation and can admit when they are wrong without any dent to their overall confidence and self-belief.

■ The above information is reprinted with kind permission from Shining Bright. Visit www.shining-bright.co.uk for more information.
© *Shining Bright*

What is low self-esteem?

Information from Shining Bright

Our self-belief – and therefore our self-esteem – is based around how we think, feel and behave. The following are examples of thoughts, feelings and behaviour which suggest a low level of self-esteem and as a consequence, an imbalanced approach to life.

People with low self-esteem tend to:

Thoughts

- Not believe themselves to be worthy
- Feel undeserving
- Have little or no self-respect
- Not be able to change or 'make things happen'
- Feel like a failure and powerless to do any better
- Feel like a victim
- Be unable to accept compliments easily.

Feelings

- Dislike themselves and can become defensive when questioned
- Be uptight and demonstrate either self-doubt or arrogance
- Be devastated by criticism
- Be unforgiving of their own mistakes and critical of the mistakes of others
- Have an imbalanced and negative approach to life
- Feel demotivated and unable to see a clear path for improvement
- Feel insecure or inadequate and worry about what others think
- Feel complacent about their current situation
- Put the needs of others before their own.

Behaviour

- Be indecisive
- Communicate poorly
- Criticise others to bolster themselves
- Not be able to ask for help if they need it
- Are threatened by the success and achievements of others
- Are unable to take risks
- Find it hard to say 'No'

- Be incapable of showing their feelings openly
- Be arrogant or overly forceful to overcompensate.

People with low self-esteem tend to avoid challenges and opportunities. They can be overly dependent on others but also put the needs of others before their own. They can be indecisive and self-critical which can lead to more serious conditions such as depression. People with low self-esteem can feel powerless and like a failure – undeserving of anything more positive in their lives.

- Information from Shining Bright. Visit www.shining-bright.co.uk for more information.

© Shining Bright

Is high self-esteem a bad thing?

Information from Uncommon Knowledge

It's understandable why many people think that high self-esteem is the antidote to low self-esteem. In life generally, if you have too little money, lots of money is attractive. If you don't have enough food, a banquet is highly appealing.

But you need to think about high self-esteem differently. Self-esteem is more like paracetamol – the right amount will help you, but too much is a very bad idea indeed.

Truly low self-esteem is a terrible thing; having the opinion that you yourself are worthless – are rubbish – is a condition no one should have to endure. But high self-esteem is a serious obstacle too, if not for you, then certainly for those around you.

Some characterstics of people with high self-esteem are:
- Being prone to self-satisfied boasting
- Tending to be smug and superior
- Abusing relationships, assuming their needs come first in any situation. If this doesn't happen, they will become angry and bullying
- Adopting an air of superiority, simply because they have skill or luck in a particular area of life
- Being blind to their own faults and so are unlikely to change or improve themselves
- Tending to have impulse control problems.

There is also now a wealth of evidence linking high self-esteem to criminality.

I often hear clients suffering from real low self-esteem compare themselves with the swaggering, loud uber-confident lad at their school, or the superman in their boardroom, but that does them no justice at all. I would much rather spend time with someone who has lower self-esteem than someone with super-high self-esteem – they are generally just nicer people!

Understanding that that super-confident individual has a handicap as real as their own can make a great difference to the way they feel about themselves.

With self-esteem, as with so much in life, balance is everything.
Article by Roger Elliott, author of the Free Self Confidence Course.

- The above information is reprinted with kind permission from Uncommon Knowledge Ltd. Visit www.self-confidence.co.uk for more information.

© Uncommon Knowledge Ltd

Mistaken ways of thinking

The following list gives examples of thinking errors that often go along with low self-esteem and eating problems. See if you recognise any! If you do, perhaps you can work on helping yourself to change them.

Feelings are facts

An example of this mistaken idea can be seen in people with an eating disorder who often feel disgusted with themselves and their bodies, so believe that in reality they must be disgusting or fat.

Black and white thinking

This arises when people or situations are only seen in extreme terms – all or nothing, black or white. The person with the eating problem may see themselves as either extremely thin and needing to starve to stay like that, or that if they eat, they will become hugely fat.

Negative thinking

This is when the person can only focus on the negative, the down side of a problem or situation, and sets aside the positive aspects. They then worry obsessively about what they see as negative things.

Won't see the positive side

Here the positive aspects of ourselves are not taken into account, made smaller and less important. Talents, qualities and successes are viewed as 'one-offs', or 'lucky'. As a result, the person is robbed of the positive self-esteem growth that would result from accepting their successes. Little or no pride is taken in these positive experiences.

Self-critical statements

These are the type of thoughts which repeatedly tell us what we 'should' or 'should not' be thinking, or feeling and behaving. These statements come from our own 'inner critic'. They are rigid and demanding and often unreasonable. They can cause us a great deal of stress and can often make our life a misery.

Blaming yourself

This is when we falsely blame ourselves for everything that goes wrong in our lives, or around us, no matter what it is. We may feel personally responsible for others' mistakes and may feel guilty, even when we know we are, in reality, completely innocent.

Over-generalisation

This is when you think that because one thing doesn't work out, that it is never going to work out in the future, e.g. a girl is stood up on a date and so decides (falsely) that all men must be unreliable and will let her down.

Jumping to conclusions

This is a form of negative thinking when you think the worst about yourself or a particular situation; continuing from above, if you're stood up on a date, then it must be to do with you and so will happen again, that you don't deserve anything better.

Tagging

This is where you tag, or label yourself or another in a negative way on the basis of one misjudgement or error. E.g. on the basis of one small mistake, you may label yourself as a 'bad, selfish person'.

'Calamity Jane' thinking

All dramas are turned into crises! Small problems become major disasters. Bad disaster movie scenarios run through the mind as soon as one small thing happens.

Ten proven ways to increase happiness and self-esteem

1. You are a worthwhile, wonderful, capable, loveable person: your task is to get in touch with this reality about yourself until you really feel it.
2. Get in touch with positive feelings. Think about things you have done and the times you've felt valued. Every time you start taking a trip down misery lane remind yourself you are worthy. Cancel negative self-talk.
3. List things you can do and the positive qualities about yourself. Learning to swim, cycle or dance, or studying and passing exams. List those things you regard as achievements, even if they were not approved of by other people.
4. Get in touch with your purpose! It helps to be clear about what is important in life. Set yourself goals and a realistic time in which you want to achieve them.
5. Learn from negative experiences. When something goes wrong, ask yourself, what can I learn from this? If something similar happens again, what would I do? Stand back and look at the actions as if someone else did them – a friend, perhaps – what would you suggest they do? If the feelings are too painful then put them aside until you have the strength or support to deal with them. On no account should you punish yourself; you did the best you could do at the time. Learn something positive from a horrible experience.
6. Get closer to friends and the people you love. Express your feelings. Practise being a good talker and listener. Close relationships are built on good communication.
7. Choose something connected with what you want to do at this moment; it may be an assertiveness course, an art or dance class or drama group. The main thing is to do something with people who are capable of valuing you. Find people who give you encouraging feedback.
8. Don't live in the problem, live in the solution. Bring your problems out in the open, and with the help of others, find constructive ways of sorting them out. Look out some self-help books and tapes. Find something that suits you, and use it!
9. Get close to nature.
10. If you're feeling down try these quick fixes: listen to music, pay someone a compliment, show your appreciation of others, say thank you, smile, give yourself a little treat.

■ Information reprinted with kind permission from the Eating Disorders Association. Visit www.edauk.com for more information.

© Eating Disorders Association

Top ten facts about low self-esteem

Information from Uncommon Knowledge Ltd

By Mark Tyrrell

Late in 2001, thinking about 'low self-esteem' changed worldwide. The Rowntree Report (*The costs and causes of low self-esteem*) paved the way for more effective, research-based identification and treatment of low self-esteem.

If you suffer from low self-esteem (or have been told you do), or treat people with low self-esteem (or think you do), please read on.

Mark Tyrrell, co-author of the *Self Confidence Trainer*, completed UK tours in 2002, 2003, 2004 and 2005 teaching thousands of health professionals the facts about self-esteem and how to treat low self-esteem in their patients. He has also co-authored a book on self-esteem for Axis Publishing called *The Giant Within – Maximise Your Self-esteem.*

As you can imagine, Mark did a lot of research for his seminar 'How to Lift Low Self-esteem'. He has listed his 10 most important 'Tips' for you here.

1) Low self-esteem not to blame!

We now know that all the ills of society cannot be blamed on low-self-esteem (Prof Nicholas Emler – The Rowntree Report 2001). According to the latest research, low self-esteem

is not to blame for nearly as many problems as has traditionally been thought.

2) High self-esteem linked to criminality

It is now clear that too high self-esteem or 'High Self-esteem Disorder' is often more of a problem. (This is NOT merely a 'disguised' form of low self-esteem, as commonly thought.) So, if you are the victim of a bully then you can rest assured you don't have to feel sorry for them.

Hundreds of pieces of reliable research now show that bullies and many criminals are much more likely to suffer from unrealistically high self-esteem and impulse control problems than low self-esteem. An exaggerated sense of entitlement – expecting much from many situations – is more likely to lead to frustration and aggressive, antisocial, or even criminal behaviour.

3) A little more uncertainty can help

Contrary to popular opinion, people with low self-esteem are always very sure of themselves.

This manifests in their conviction that they are worthless or inadequate. As you will know if you have ever tried to argue with someone who puts themselves down continually, it is very hard to do! When someone with low self-esteem becomes less sure of their own opinion of themselves and therefore begins to assess counter evidence regarding their worthlessness, their self-image begins to become more healthy.

4) You can't argue someone better!

Telling someone they are great or wonderful when they are constantly negative about themselves will not work. Arguing with someone who is so sure of themselves does not work, as we all know. You will just break rapport with that person. We have all met people who feel more comfortable in relationships with people who treat them badly – because that person seems to see things the way they do.

People with low self-esteem can be upset by 'disconfirming feedback'. In other words if something happens which indicates that they may not be as terrible as they thought, it can feel disturbing as it contradicts their way of perceiving. Healthy self-esteem needs to emerge subtly, not as a sudden result of hearing you are 'really special' or 'fantastic'.

People need proof that unsettles the certainty that they are so 'defective' or inadequate and leads to a more realistic and balanced self-assessment. This can only happen when they become calmer and more relaxed so that they can observe themselves more objectively and less emotionally. Whenever we are highly emotional our perception is distorted ('emotional hijacking'), when people calm down around the idea of themselves then a healthier self-esteem can emerge!

5) Child abuse increases likelihood of low self-esteem

People who were abused as children (physical beating or sexual abuse) are more likely to suffer unrealistic low self-esteem as adults. This is because of constant repetition of a 'message' that they are of little value or just an object to be used. In a way they have been 'brainwashed' by constant criticism or abuse that they are a certain way.

When a person begins to question this former conditioning or brainwashing then a healthier and more accurate sense of self can begin to emerge. However, the person may have to be de-traumatised so the emotional brain responds differently in future (rather than solely learning to think differently about stuff). However, the way we think and our assumptions need to be observed, understood and if necessary challenged.

(Note: Most people who have low self-esteem were not abused as children.)

6) Healthy pleasures are vital

We need to engage in activities which we enjoy and in which we can 'lose ourselves' regularly. The better one's sense of themselves the less they tend to use words like 'me, myself, I, mine' (personal pronouns). Someone's mental and even, to some extent, physical health can be directly related to how 'self-referential' they are in their conversation – as people become healthier they use the 'I' word less, in the same way that when your knee stops hurting you don't need to rub it any more.

> **To change your self-image and improve low self-esteem, you need to believe in an alternative opinion of yourself, not just repeat platitudes about how great you are really**

People should be encouraged to focus their attention away from themselves as well as to be able to take their own needs into account. A healthy balance should be encouraged as should the development of real practical skills. Real responsibility should be encouraged so that self-worth can respond to external evidence on an ongoing basis.

7) Make the most of success

Low self-esteem requires a particular attitude towards success. Whenever you succeed at something, you must 'write it off' as good luck, chance, or someone else's responsibility.

To gain a more realistic view of yourself, you need to take appropriate credit for your successes. In the *Self Confidence Trainer*, we call this skill 'Converting'.

This involves learning how to convert real successes into statements about yourself. The other part of the picture is to view perceived failures as temporary and not statements about your 'core identity'.

8) Build on solid foundations

For anyone to be psychologically and physically healthy on an ongoing basis, there are a set of requirements that must be built into life. This is the checklist I use with my patients:

1. The need to give and receive attention
2. Taking care of the mind-body connection
3. The need for meaning, purpose and goals
4. The need for a connection to something greater than ourselves
5. The need for creativity and stimulation
6. The need for intimacy and connection
7. The need for a sense of control
8. The need for status.

Of course, it is likely that at any one time, one or more of these may be slightly lacking in your life, without dire consequences. However, in the long-term, they must all be catered for one way or another.

9) Characteristics of genuinely low self-esteem

1. Social withdrawal
2. Anxiety and emotional turmoil
3. Lack of social skills and self-confidence. Depression and/or bouts of sadness
4. Less social conformity
5. Eating disorders
6. Inability to accept compliments
7. An inability to see yourself 'squarely' – to be fair to yourself
8. Accentuating the negative
9. Exaggerated concern over what they imagine other people think
10. Self-neglect
11. Treating yourself badly but NOT other people
12. Worrying whether you have treated others badly
13. Reluctance to take on challenges
14. Reluctance to trust your own opinion
15. Expect little out of life for yourself.

10) It's not just about positive thinking!

Positive thinking can be useful in that it challenges you to form a different view on things. However, most of the time it just takes the form of arguing with yourself, and as we've seen from 4) above, this doesn't work.

To change your self-image and improve low self-esteem, you need to believe in an alternative opinion of yourself, not just repeat platitudes about how great you are really!

Article by Mark Tyrrell, co-author of the Self Confidence Trainer.

■ The above information is reprinted with kind permission from Uncommon Knowledge Ltd. Visit www.self-confidence.co.uk for more.
© Uncommon Knowledge Ltd

Self-esteem questionnaire

Do you think you may suffer from low self-esteem? This questionnaire will help you find out. Low self-esteem (LSE) is often misunderstood, and it is even misdiagnosed by many therapists as being a secondary concern. Rather than being merely a symptom, LSE is frequently the root cause of many psychological, emotional, personal and relationship issues. Treatments that do not focus on recovery from LSE may not be effective, because they are not dealing with the core issue.

1. I generally feel anxious in new social situations where I may not know what is expected of me.

2. I find it difficult to hear criticism about myself.

3. I fear being made to look like a fool.

4. I tend to magnify my mistakes and minimise my successes.

5. I am very critical of myself and others.

6. I have periods in which I feel devastated and/or depressed.

7. I am anxious and fearful much of the time.

8. When someone mistreats me I think that I must have done something to deserve it.

9. I have difficulty knowing who to trust and when to trust.

10. I often feel like I don't know the right thing to do or say.

11. I am very concerned about my appearance.

12. I am easily embarrassed.

13. I think others are very focused on – and critical of – what I say and do.

14. I fear making a mistake which others might see.

15. I often feel depressed about things I've said and done, or things I failed to say or do.

16. I have avoided making changes in my life because I was fearful of making a mistake or failing.

17. I often get defensive and strike back when I perceive I am being criticised.

18. I have not accomplished what I am capable of due to fear and avoidance.

19. I tend to let fear and anxiety control many of my decisions.

20. I tend to think negatively much of the time.

21. I have found it difficult to perform adequately or without embarrassment when involved in sex.

22. I'm one of the following: The person who reveals too much personal information about myself or the person who seldom reveals personal information.

23. I often get so anxious that I don't know what to say.

24. I often procrastinate.

25. I try to avoid conflict and confrontation.

26. I've been told I'm too sensitive.

27. I felt inferior or inadequate as a child.

28. I tend to think that I have higher standards than others.

29. I often feel like I don't know what is expected of me.

30. I often compare myself to others.

31. I frequently think negative thoughts about myself and others.

32. I often feel that others mistreat me and/or take advantage of me.

33. At night, I frequently review my day, analysing what I said and did or what others said and did to me that day.

34. I often make decisions on the basis of what would please others rather than on what I want or without even considering what I want.

35. I often think that others don't respect me.

36. I often refrain from sharing my opinions, my ideas, and my feelings in groups.

37. I sometimes lie when I feel that the truth would result in criticism or rejection.

38. I'm fearful that I will say or do something that will make me look stupid or incompetent.

39. I do not set goals for the future.

40. I am easily discouraged.

41. I am not very aware of my feelings.

42. I grew up in a dysfunctional home.

43. I think life is harder for me than for most other people.

44. I often avoid situations where I think I will be uncomfortable.

45. I tend to be a perfectionist, needing to look perfect and to do things perfectly.

46. I feel too embarrassed to eat out alone or to attend movies or other activities by myself.

47. I often find myself angry or hurt by the behaviour and words of others.

48. At times I get so anxious or upset that I experience most of the following: heart racing or pounding, sweating, tearfulness, blushing, difficulty swallowing or lump in my throat, shaking, poor concentration, dizziness, nausea or diarrhoea, butterflies.

49. I am very fearful of criticism, disapproval or rejection.

50. I rely on the opinion of others to make decisions.

Your score

0-4 statements ticked – You have fairly good self-esteem

5-10 statements ticked – You have mild low self-esteem

11-18 statements ticked – You have moderately low self-esteem

19-50 statements ticked – You have severely low self-esteem

It's important to realise that your score on this questionnaire in no way indicates that you are not a quality person. Instead what it does is to measure how you view yourself. If you have a healthy view of yourself, your score will be low. If your view of yourself is unhealthy, your score will be high.

By Marilyn J Sorensen, PhD, Clinical Psychologist and Author. Adapted from her book, Breaking the Chain of Low Self-Esteem.

Body image and self-esteem

Information from Soul Food

Everybody has a body image – that is, we all have some sort of idea of how our body looks and is perceived by others. The relationship we have between our thoughts and our physical being is one of the most significant relationships we have during our lives.

When we are young, body image gets complicated, especially during adolescence, when our bodies begin to really change. Adolescents are often oversensitive towards their bodies during the onset of puberty. The overexposure to the media directs young people to examine their bodies and even measure their physical appearance against unrealistic computer-enhanced images.

Adolescent years are often full of confusion, self-doubt and the search for an identity, compounded by dramatic physical changes taking place in the body.

Most of us focus on things we don't like about our bodies. We tend to totally overlook the fact that we have good bits as well. If we say negative things often enough to ourselves we really start to believe them and in turn find it even harder to say something in praise of ourselves.

Seeing your body in a positive way, will improve your outlook and how you respond to other people.

Remember, until you learn to respect your body as much as your mind, behaviour and attitudes, you will never wholly respect yourself.

The benefits

- You'll glow with inner confidence, feel good about yourself and accept that even a most precious diamond has flaws.
- You'll know you are unique and will therefore stop comparing yourself to anyone else (especially supermodels).
- You'll say goodbye to 'bad hair days'. No longer will spots or unruly hair rule your mood, turning potential good times into nightmares.
- You'll no longer be so critical of your friends. By accepting that everyone is unique and by being proud of yourself, you will stop being 'Little Miss/Mister Critical'.
- You'll become more comfortable around others and no longer hide behind chairs worrying that

someone, will notice you. Instead you'll be mingling and making chit-chat.
- 'Get thin fads' and crash diets will pass you by. Your body is a temple and you'll do nothing to harm it.
- Words will never hurt you again. Those nasty uncaring comments that once would have made you cry for a week will no longer bother you. Because you are more level-headed you'll accept fair criticism, when you recognise it's for your own good.

What causes an image problem?

Poor body image can be brought about in lots of different ways and under the influence of key people in our lives e.g. parents, friends, boyfriends/girlfriends. It can also be caused by those whose main interest is self-interest e.g. media and diet industry.

What can you do about your self-image today?

The first step in dealing with low self-image is to realise that there are things that you can change and things you can't.

Make a list of the things you can change and the things you can't change. Develop an action plan to help you work on the things you can change. Set yourself realistic goals and work at your own pace to achieve these goals.

If you make a decision to change something you dislike, remember the following:
- It won't make all your other problems disappear.
- It won't happen overnight.
- If your plan does not work first time try again.
- Working towards your goal at your own pace is more likely to end in success.

The things which can't be changed are a fundamental part of you. You can choose to accept them or choose to let them get you down. By accepting them, this won't mean that you'll become instantly and blissfully happy, but it will mean that you can stop blaming the 'unchangeables' for all your misfortunes.

Reinforcing the good

On a big sheet of paper write down all your good points and don't let false modesty hold you back. Pin this list above the mirror in your room, read it regularly and update it. Take a good look at your list and imagine that someone else had all these traits.

Would you like them?

Would you want to be friends with them?

Of course you would.

Accepting who you are 'warts and all' will increase your self-esteem and give you:

- A firm belief in your own abilities.
- A feeling that you've got something to offer the world.

The overexposure to the media directs young people to examine their bodies and even measure their physical appearance against unrealistic computer-enhanced images

- A positive attitude that you can be and do whatever you work at.
- The strength to resist those who may try to control your life.

- Inner beliefs in yourself so the comments and opinions of others won't get you down.
- The courage to overcome fear of failure.

Finally remember!

- If you like yourself you will like others.
- If you respect yourself you will respect others.
- If you accept nothing is perfect, you won't ask for perfection in others.
- To make the world a better place you have to start with yourself and work outwards.

Adapted from: Self-Esteem Learn to Believe in Yourself by Anita Naik.

- The above information is reprinted with kind permission from Soul Food. Visit www.goodhealthinfo.org.uk/SoulFood for more information.

© *Soul Food*

Body image

Lorraine Smith explains the pressures the media put on women to be thin and beautiful

Shortly after Christmas I was feeling fat, which is not an unusual occurrence but was actually justified at the time due to the amount of calories I had consumed over the previous few weeks. I was also feeling old and unfashionable due to an evening spent in a pub packed with people between 4 and 10 years younger than me who were wearing outfits purchased in the last 4 months, as opposed to the last 4 years.

the f word
contemporary UK feminism

Although there's no real pressure on me to conform to a young, thin and fashionable stereotype, I still find myself occasionally wishing I was something other than I am. Most of the time I am quite happy with the way I look. I know I have a big bottom and would love to have longer legs but there's no point in worrying about things I have little hope of ever changing, as I will just end up feeling depressed and overcome by feelings of self-doubt. I've never been one to look at photos in magazines and fret that I don't match up to the image of apparent perfection that they portray, as they are generally airbrushed pictures of unusual-looking models, but I have recently noticed that I *am* actually affected by images on television and in magazines.

Research by the University of Glasgow suggested that women are up to ten times more likely than men to be unhappy with their body image

I didn't realise just how few media images there are of women I can relate to until one television advert really made me smile. It was for the Nokia 7650 where three men expose their bellies to wish happy birthday to a colleague, who then takes a picture with her phone. It's full of normal-looking people just being themselves which is rare in today's media, and even more so in advertising.

Why do so many rational women have body image problems? Research by the University of Glasgow suggested that women are up to ten times more likely than men to be unhappy with their body image. Why is this? Who is putting pressure on us to be young and thin? You don't have to go too far to find an answer

Sometimes I wonder if women are in fact their own worst enemy when it comes to the poor image they have of their own body

to this question: just as far as your television set, in fact. When we're not being bombarded with images of tall, slender and glamorous young women in programmes where all the fat characters are there for comedy value only, we then get subjected to adverts for Weight Watchers and Slim Fast during the commercial breaks. OK so, no one has told us that we simply *must* buy these products in order to look like these people, but it doesn't help when you go shopping for clothes only to find that nothing fits.

So-called 'fashionable' retailers skimp on fabric so their sizes come up smaller, and they shape their

garments for a more athletic figure than the majority of women have. This means that a lot of women feel abnormal when they are in fact quite the opposite, and it is affecting us at a younger age than ever before. Teenagers have always been teased at school for looking fatter, thinner, taller or shorter than their peers but, as the magazine market for young girls increases and the desire to grow up kicks in at earlier ages than ever before, young women are finding it more and more difficult to accept the way they look. A survey of 500 school pupils by the Young Women's Christian Association revealed that one in three thought about their body shape all the time and only 14% were happy with the way they look.

Television companies, clothing retailers, magazine editors, advertising agencies and Hollywood should all really do more to halt this trend. We need images of women whom we can aspire to be like, but not simply because they look a certain way. After all, there's more to glamour than looking good in a bikini. Jamie Lee Curtis posed sans make-up and photo re-touching for a magazine last year, then Kate Winslet destroyed all her earlier good work and caused outrage earlier this year with her blatantly airbrushed cover for a men's mag.

Every now and again someone in the media mentions that there is a problem (remember British *Vogue*'s

shoot with a size 14 model?), only to merrily sweep it back under the carpet again once they have cashed in. Perhaps we shouldn't wait for the media to catch up and should focus on ourselves first, but it's tricky to 'love the skin you're in' when you're constantly being told that you have too much of the damn stuff in the first place.

The thing that bothers me the most about all this, however, is that men are not under the same pressure to conform. Although there is evidence to suggest that men are becoming more obsessed with their appearance than ever before (usually by being urged to replace their keg with a six-pack if they want to impress us), society accepts a far wider variety of male body shapes than female. Men are still adored by their girlfriends/wives when they pile on the pounds, but then find these same women unattractive if they happen to go up a couple of dress sizes. Men can go without shaving and still feel sexy, but a woman misplaces her razor and all hell breaks loose! Men can grow old gracefully, whereas women are constantly being told that wrinkles are bad and will make you look like an extra for *Last of the Summer Wine* before you're thirty if you don't spend at least fifteen quid on a pot of cream.

I suspect that social conditioning has a lot to do with this, but most men do seem to be immune to the media images of sultry male models draped in young girls, preferring instead just to look at the girls. Buy a women's magazine and you will see pictures of the young and slender women that, in someone's ideal world, we are all supposed to look like. Buy a copy of a men's magazine, however, and you will see photos of the same women. There may be men on the fashion pages, but the readers will doubtless be looking at just the clothes by this point. Why can't we do that? Sometimes I wonder if women are in fact their own worst enemy when it comes to the poor image they have of their own body.

■ Information from The F-Word. Visit www.thefword.org.uk for more information.

© *The F-Word*

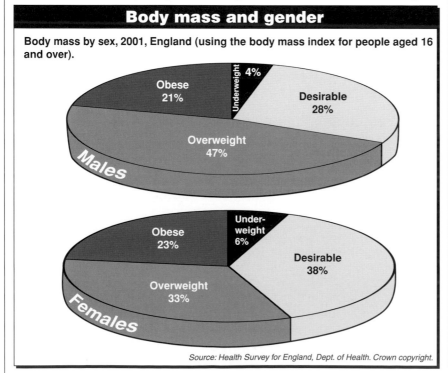

Body mass and gender

Body mass by sex, 2001, England (using the body mass index for people aged 16 and over).

Males
Underweight 4%
Desirable 28%
Overweight 47%
Obese 21%

Females
Underweight 6%
Desirable 38%
Overweight 33%
Obese 23%

Source: Health Survey for England, Dept. of Health. Crown copyright.

The Dove Self-Esteem Fund

Whether it's models that wear a size 6 or movie stars with exceptional curves, beauty pressures are everywhere. And when young girls find it hard to keep up, low self-esteem can take over

Why did we create the Dove Self-Esteem Fund?

- Over 50% of women say their body disgusts them (*Dove Internal Study, 2002*)
- The body fat of models and actresses portrayed in the media is at least 10% less than that of healthy women (*British Medical Association, 2000*)
- 6 out of 10 girls think they'd be happier if they were thinner (*UK Teen Body Image Survey, Jan 2004*)
- While only 19% of teenage girls are 'overweight', 67% think they 'need to lose weight' (*UK Teen Body Image Survey, Jan 2004*)

Low self-esteem leads to introversion, a withdrawal from normal life and a waste of potential. The Dove Self-Esteem Fund was created to support different initiatives that help educate and inspire girls on a wider definition of beauty.

How it works

The Dove Self-Esteem Fund has already been put to work in many parts of the world. Here are a few success stories.

In the United Kingdom
BodyTalk

There are 1.1 million people with an eating disorder in the UK and young women aged 14-25 are most likely to be affected. The Eating Disorders Association (EDA) knows that building self-esteem and a positive body image can help reduce those risks.

With the aid of the Dove Self-Esteem Fund, EDA has developed *BodyTalk*, a workshop designed to help young girls (and boys) understand and deal with feelings about their physical appearance, and learn how 'ideal' images of beauty are created.

Over 3 years, *BodyTalk* aims to:
- Address the National Curriculum

and Health Education for 12 to 14-year-olds
- Reach over 8,000 pupils through workshop sessions
- Give more than 200 teachers the skills and educational materials to continue the *BodyTalk* workshops in their schools.

In Canada
Beyond Compare Photo Tour

Photographers from around the world were recently asked to participate in Beyond Compare – a photographic show that would raise money for the National Eating Disorder Information Centre (NEDIC). The result? Sixty-seven photographs were donated, raising a grand total of $21,000 Canadian.

The Dove Self-Esteem Fund has helped make the tour possible and, in total, is responsible for already raising over $50,000 Canadian for NEDIC in 2004. NEDIC plans to use some of these funds to build an e-module with self-esteem information and guidance for 12 to 14-year-old girls.

In the Netherlands
Beyond Compare Photo Tour

The Beyond Compare Photo Tour has made its way to the Netherlands and, since June 2004, has already raised thousands of Euros, via donations, for Kenniscentrum Eetstoornissen Nederland – a leading charity in the fight against eating disorders in the Netherlands.

- The above information is reprinted with kind permission from Unilever. Visit www.campaignforrealbeauty. co.uk for more information.

© Unilever

How can we learn to love our bodies?

Information from Channel 4

By Jenny Bryan

Seven-year-old Ellen squeezes an inch of flesh over the top of her jeans to show how fat she is and complains about the state of her legs:

'I think people think I'm fat because I'm the only one in my class that has got fat legs. Everyone else has got skinny legs,' she lisps through the gap in her front teeth.

At 11, her older sister Laura is already taking action against what she sees as her fat tummy by doing step ups and sits ups at night before she goes to bed. Yet her skinny frame has yet to register any sign of the increase in body fat that goes with puberty.

> *From an early age, children link being fat with being unintelligent, doing less well at school, being lazy and smelly and less liked by parents*

Ellen and Laura's mother, Paula, claims never to have dieted seriously but, as Ellen reports, she uses slimming drinks to keep her weight down.

Six-year-old Vanessa's mum feels guilty that her daughter already worries about her 'fat' thighs when she wears a bikini and wants to lose some weight.

'I just think that my bad self-image has rubbed off on my daughter and I don't know how to combat that. I don't know how to redress it and I'm really concerned for the future,' she explains.

Body dissatisfaction is now so common amongst girls and women of all ages that psychologists are beginning to question whether it's even an illness. Women who are asked to point to pictures that most closely resemble the shape and size of their body routinely pick women who are larger than themselves.

'Eighty-five to ninety per cent of women overestimate their size, so can we still say that problems with body image are pathological if they affect nearly half the population?' asks Professor Glenn Waller, head of clinical psychology at St George's Hospital, London.

Dr Andrew Hill, from Leeds University Medical School, explains that body image problems are often passed down through families:

'If mum's concerned about her weight and if there are siblings who are dieting, then younger children are also likely to be shape- and weight-concerned, and dieting themselves. There's some sort of transmission within the family,' he says.

'There are five-year-olds who are acutely aware of what dieting means. It's almost like using nutrition as a scalpel. You can trim bits off your body, lose a bit of weight and achieve the body shape you want, simple by reducing the amount that you eat,' he adds.

His research shows that, from an early age, children link being fat with being unintelligent, doing less well at school, being lazy and smelly and less liked by parents. In contrast, skinny shapes are associated with being successful and attractive and having lots of friends.

The body haters

White, heterosexual women in the higher social classes, living in westernised countries, are most dissatisfied with their size and shape; income, it appears, is less of a factor.

Most men have largely escaped the burden of body image, though gay men record significant problems with body satisfaction and self-esteem.

Exposure to images of successful, thin female actresses, models and other celebrities from an early age is widely blamed for our growing dissatisfaction with our bodies.

'Western society idealises extreme thinness and this impacts on women's body image by becoming a source of comparison for making judgements about the body,' explains Dr Sarah Grogan, principal lecturer in health psychology at Staffordshire University.

Twelve-year-old Jung has a south-east Asian appearance, yet she yearns to look like German supermodel Claudia Schiffer. She is 7 stone and trying to lose a stone in weight by dieting, skipping, and running around the block every night until her legs hurt. She even does facial exercises to try to take weight off her face.

'I know my face doesn't look anything like Claudia Schiffer but perhaps my body could look like Claudia Schiffer if I try,' she says.

Vulnerable women

A recent review of 25 studies with nearly 2,300 women confirmed that looking at pictures of thin models has a negative impact on body image compared with looking at pictures of average or large models, or inanimate objects. Women under the age of 19 and those who already felt less good about their body were worst affected by looking at the images of thin women.

In one recent body image study, half of the 219 young women who took part were rewarded with a 15-month subscription to a teen women's magazine. Overall, reading articles about losing weight and looking good had little effect on the group's body image. But those who were dissatisfied with their appearance at the start of the study felt even worse about themselves by the time they'd read 15 issues of the magazine.

'Media exposure alone won't necessarily make women dissatisfied about their body. What is important is the interaction between vulnerable people and the media,' points out Dr Hill.

Among the most vulnerable are those who mentally 'buy into' or internalise socially defined ideals of attractiveness which are then reinforced by peer groups, families and role models, explains Dr Hill. People who internalise the thin-ideal are more likely to be dissatisfied with their own body, to diet and to develop bulimic symptoms.

Also vulnerable are those who routinely compare themselves with people who are more attractive or thinner than themselves. These are often adolescent girls who perceive themselves as unattractive and are lacking in self-esteem.

'We have a natural drive for self-evaluation, but most of us want to feel good about ourselves and tend to make downward comparisons with people who have less money and do not have such a good life. Body dissatisfaction comes from continual upward comparisons with people who are more attractive and thinner,' says Dr Hill.

Clues to greater resilience

Ironically, obese and overweight children who don't care how they look may be able to provide some clues to helping those whose dissatisfaction about their body makes their life a misery. Some overweight children are remarkably resilient to society's current obsession with thin, well-toned bodies. They may blame their weight problem on factors beyond their control or they may discount its importance. Their perception of their size and shape may be distorted so they think they are thinner than they are. Helping vulnerable children to develop similar coping skills may make them more resilient to society's pressures to be thin.

Preventing body dissatisfaction

Efforts to 'immunise' vulnerable young people against the impact of media images have focused on helping adolescents to analyse and become more aware of the messages contained in such images and to relate them to their own feelings and expectations. Such efforts may work in the short term, but the longer-term outcomes are far less encouraging. Long-term behavioural changes have been reported in only 3 out of 15 studies.

White, heterosexual women in the higher social classes, living in westernised countries, are most dissatisfied with their size and shape

---

For example, in Australia, a school-based programme tried to improve body image and self-esteem amongst mainly girls aged 11-14. Initially, attitudes improved and only 2% of girls were dieting, compared to 8% of a control group who didn't take part in the programme. But, a year later, there was a reversal, with 9% of the girls in the programme trying to lose weight compared to 6% of those in the control group.

Other studies have shown that it is possible to reduce internalisation of the thin-ideal but this doesn't automatically change body dissatisfaction.

Prevention programmes for eating disorders have produced equally mixed results and some specialists

are concerned that well-meaning educational schemes in schools can do more harm than good.

'Primary prevention can introduce people to beliefs and attitudes that lead to eating disorders. They can glamorise and normalise eating disorders to young girls,' explains Dr Roz Shafran, from the department of psychiatry at Oxford University. 'If you educate people you can increase their knowledge but there is no change in their dieting and weight loss behaviour,' she adds.

Despite the disappointments, some psychologists remain optimistic that, if educational programmes are targeted towards the right population of vulnerable young girls, they should be able to change body dissatisfaction and prevent the depression and eating disorders which so often accompany it. The reality is that, as yet, there is precious little evidence that this is the case. Until more effective interventions can be developed, all the specialists can do is try to pick up the pieces after those who go on to develop anorexia or bulimia recognise that they have a problem and can be persuaded to do something about it.

■ The above information is re-printed with kind permission from Channel 4. Visit www.channel4.com for more information.

© Channel 4

Female body image timeline

Every culture has its own beauty ideals, and every period of history held its own standards on what was and was not considered beautiful. TheSite maps it all out

Western society

Western society is intensely pre-occupied with body size, exerting enormous pressure on individuals to conform to the thin ideal of body weight. This influence is imposed upon children, adolescents, and adults. Although the ideal for men has changed to encourage a more muscular, lean frame, the focus of the extreme messages and pressures has been on females. The ideal shape tends to be whatever is most difficult to achieve during a given time period. If too many women were able to meet the ideal, then standards would have to change for the ideal to retain its extraordinary nature. Even worse is that the ideal shape is becoming harder and harder to achieve as time goes on.

The major change across time in Western culture is the degree to which we are concerned. Previously a mild concern to look nice was fair enough, however mass culture and the media have served to project the body ideal and turn gentle concern into obsessions, and dangerous ones at that. The media have given us very rigid, uniform beauty ideals. TV, magazines, billboards mean we see beautiful people more often than we

TheSite.org

see members of our family, the ideal becomes more familiar to us than our friends and thus appears normal and attainable.

The history of ideal female body shape

1800s to present day

During the Victorian era, the ideal body type for women was plump, fleshy, and full-figured. They wore restrictive corsets, which made waists artificially tiny while accentuating the hips and buttocks. These corsets also caused a variety of health problems with breathing and digestion.

1900s-1950s

At the start of the 1900s, slenderness became more fashionable. There was an increasing interest of women in athletics and physicians began to see body weight as a 'science' of calorie counting, 'ideal weights', and weigh-ins. At this time the physically perfect woman was 5'4" tall and weighed 10 stone.

By the 1920s, the Victorian hourglass gave way to the thin flapper who bound her breasts to achieve a washboard profile. After World War I, active lifestyles added another dimension. Energy and vitality became central and body fat was perceived to contribute to inefficiency and was seen as a sign of self-indulgence. By the 1950s, a thin woman with a large bust line was considered most attractive. The voluptuous (size 16) Marilyn Monroe set a new standard for women who now needed to rebuild the curves they had previously tried to bind and restrain.

Western society is intensely preoccupied with body size, exerting enormous pressure on individuals to conform to the thin ideal of body weight

1960s-1990s

By the 1960s, slenderness became the most important indicator of physical attractiveness following the arrival of model Twiggy. She weighed in at a shapeless six and a half stones, and had the figure of a prepubescent boy.

Despite an American public with increasing body weights, *Playboy* magazine increased the promotion of slimness between 1959 and 1978. 'Miss America' contestants were also found to be thinner over time, and winners of the pageant after 1970 consistently weighed less than the other contestants. In 1975 top

models and beauty queens weighed only 8% less than the average woman. Today they weigh 23% less, a size achievable by less than 5% of today's female population. Between 1970 and 1990, there was an overall increased emphasis on weight loss and body shape in the content of a popular women's magazine, as well as a shift to using thinner, less curvaceous models in their photo shoots. The 1980s beauty ideal remained slim but required a more toned and fit look. Women could

> *Today in our Western society, 'thin is in' and artificial means have been used to lessen the appearance of fat*

no longer just 'diet' into the correct size; there was a new pressure to add exercise to achieve the toned look. The 1990s body ideal was very slim and large-breasted, think Pamela 'Baywatch' Anderson, an almost impossible combination for most western women.

Looking forwards

Today in our modern Western society, 'thin is in' and artificial means such as liposuction have sometimes been used to lessen the appearance of hips, buttocks and fat in general.

The future seems bleak, unless we reverse the trend and see big as beautiful once again. Who really wants a society full of animated anorexics with gravity-defying breasts? Not TheSite, that's for sure.

■ Information from TheSite.org. Please visit www.thesite.org for more information.

© *TheSite.org*

Eating disorders, body image and the media

A summary from the British Medical Association

■ Eating disorders are a significant cause of mortality and morbidity in young people, particularly young women. Even if young people recover from an eating disorder, they may suffer long-term health problems as a result of their illness.

■ Eating disorders are caused by a complex interplay between genetics, family history and the cultural environment.

■ Social factors implicated in the development of eating disorders include sociocultural norms regarding thinness, eating, food preparation and roles of women.

■ The media provide particular examples of role expectations and images of beauty which may influence young people's perceptions of acceptable body image.

■ Obesity is an increasing problem in the UK, with adverse consequences for health. However, the considerable health risks for women associated with being underweight are less well publicised.

■ Dieting is an important precipitant factor in the development of eating disorders. Young women are dieting at an increasingly young age, and expressing dissatisfaction with their body shapes.

■ Many young people do not eat regular family meals and may not have positive associations with food. This may place them at risk of developing an eating disorder.

■ Eating disorders became more prevalent in Western industrialised countries in the latter part of the 20th century.

■ Fewer Asian and black women apparently suffer from eating disorders, although there are higher rates amongst immigrants to Western society and ethnic minority populations raised in Western industrialised cultures, or those following a Western model of development.

■ Eating disorders predominantly affect young women. However, evidence from studies of men with eating disorders also suggest that perceived body image measured against a societal 'norm' is a crucial factor in the onset of the illness.

■ Although certain biological predispositions (which may in part be genetically determined) may contribute to the onset of eating disorders in an individual, historical and cross-cultural evidence suggests that the development of eating disorders is significantly influenced by particular aspects of modern society.

■ The media are a significant and pervasive influence in modern society, and provide information about gender roles, fashion and acceptable body image which may be particularly influential on those young children and adolescents who are heavily exposed to its content.

- Advertising, in particular, may influence young people's perception of fashion, beauty and attitudes towards food.
- Young women may compare themselves to extremely thin models, working in the fashion industry or advertising products, and perceive themselves as 'fat' in comparison, rather than healthy and attractive.
- For eating disorder sufferers, their bodies become the means by which they judge the success of their lives. Encouraging and developing self-esteem which is not dependent upon body size may be a key to protecting vulnerable individuals from developing eating disorders.

- The media can boost self-esteem where they are providing examples of a variety of body shapes, roles and routes of achievement for young men and women. However, they often tend to portray a limited number of body shapes and messages linking external appearance with success – this is potentially damaging to the self-esteem of young people.
- The media are an important source of health care information for young people, particularly through the medium of women's magazines, and their positive contribution to health should not be underestimated. However, it is important that care and consideration is given to the messages that are conveyed by the media and received by young people.
- Primary prevention programmes for eating disorders aim to reduce risk factors for the illness and increase young people's resistance to risk factors. Changes can be made at a societal level to achieve these goals, for example, reducing exposure to media images of thin women and increasing awareness of issues relating to body image, self-esteem and pressure to diet, in the school curriculum.

- Information from the British Medical Association. Visit www. bma.org.uk for more information.

© BMA

Do you have body angst?

Start improving your self-image and confidence today

Body image involves far more than our perception of how we appear to others. It encompasses our self-esteem and self-respect, and it can impinge on everything from a decision about what dress we wear to a party to our relationships, work and health.

Studies suggest that women and men are constantly evaluating themselves, based on whether they look good and how they feel about their bodies. These studies also show a direct correlation between low self-esteem and poor body image so, in theory, by developing a better body image, we could all improve our self-confidence.

By Christina Stark

Almost the entire Western world is obsessed with image in one way or another, so it's only natural that we all focus on how we look. This tendency can become exacerbated by growing up in a family that places enormous emphasis on appearance or being at a school where thin girls are perceived as being perfect. In these circumstances, a distorted body image can be reinforced and begin to develop into an eating disorder.

You don't need to have an eating disorder to have distorted body image. Answer the questions below to see how your body image shapes up.

Are you:
- preoccupied with body shape and size or constantly weighing yourself and feeling dissatisfied with your body?
- continually seeking approval from friends about how you look, or experiencing a general feeling of insecurity about your body's appearance?
- always comparing your body to others and dwelling on your imperfections?

- frequently worrying over what to wear and hiding parts of your body you dislike?
- feeling that worrying over your body is ruining your life and causing you to feel anxious and depressed?

If you think you have a poor body image, don't panic. Only a small percentage of women develop an eating disorder as a result. And you can improve your body image. There is no quick-fix solution, but if you improve your relationship with your body, you can change your perception of it. Be proactive and persistent. Here's how to start:
- **Think holistically.** See yourself as a whole person. Refuse to judge yourself on your looks alone. You are a unique person, not just a physical body.
- **Value yourself.** List your positive traits and celebrate your achievements. Don't put yourself down or negate your strengths. Invest in yourself. You alone have the power to improve your self-esteem.
- **Reject the beauty myth.** Reject the idea that there is only one version of female beauty. Recognise that adverts are not reality. Accept your unique

- attractiveness and remember we all have imperfections.
- **Try to accept your size and shape.** This is a tough one. We are all different sizes and shapes, as a result of genetic factors that are out of our control. We can't all be size eight or ten. If you come from a family with a genetic predisposition to be overweight, you need to accept this and try to eat a healthier diet. Focus on achieving the goal of a healthy weight appropriate for your height, age, and build.

- **Set achievable goals.** Take up a realistic fitness regime, by getting advice from your GP or a local fitness instructor. Don't expect unrealistic results, and don't be too hard on yourself if you don't meet your goals or have a setback.
- **Stop comparing yourself to others.** Accept your personal strengths and limitations. Becoming comfortable with yourself and your body may be a long process, especially if you are inclined to be self-critical.

Counselling can help you come to terms with your body image and help put things in perspective.

For more information, contact the Eating Disorder Association: Adult helpline: 01603 621 414 (9am-6.30pm, Mon-Fri) Youth helpline: 01603 765 050 (4pm-6pm, Mon-Fri).

- The above information is reprinted with kind permission from iVillage. Visit www.ivillage.co.uk for more information.

© iVillage

We hate our bodies

Few British women are confident about their looks, with just one in five considering themselves attractive, a survey has revealed

Few British women are confident about their looks, with just one in five considering themselves attractive, a survey has revealed.

The research, carried out before the last few weeks of festive overindulgence, also found that a tiny one in 50 felt confident enough to describe themselves as 'sexy'.

Women in countries around the world were asked which of 12 different descriptions best matched their opinion of their appearance.

The words included 'attractive', 'beautiful', 'good-looking', 'pretty', 'stunning' and 'gorgeous'.

The women with the most positive attitude were Brazilians, 6 per cent of whom described themselves as 'beautiful'.

In contrast, 54 per cent of British women said they would feel uncomfortable with the description – the highest negative response in the poll.

The survey was carried out by the London School of Economics and Harvard University for soap and beauty products maker Dove, which tends to use fuller-figured women in its advertising.

Academics questioned 3,200 women aged between 18 and 64 in ten countries, which also included the US, Canada, Italy, France, the Netherlands, Portugal, Brazil, Argentina and Japan.

By James Tozer

Greater opportunities?

Almost half of those questioned thought that highly attractive women had greater opportunities in life.

British women were among the most concerned about their weight, with 57 per cent describing it as 'too high' – a figure topped only by the US.

Three-quarters of women in the UK wanted to see a greater range of shapes, ages and sizes portrayed in advertising and the media.

Dr Susie Orbach, psychotherapist and writer and co-author of the report, said it showed women wanted to see the idea of beauty 'expanded'.

'What women in this study tell us is that a sense of legitimacy and respect is wrapped up with beauty in today's world,' she added.

'Whether this sentiment dismays or delights us, it poses a serious challenge.'

Separate research in Britain by Dove reveals the extent to which young girls are already concerned about what constitutes beauty.

Young girls' concerns

The study, carried out by the parenting website www.raisingkids.co.uk, found that three-quarters of girls aged eight to 13 would like to change something about their appearance.

In addition, two-thirds of ten-year-old girls equated blonde hair with being beautiful, with 73 per cent adding that a key factor was being slim and 83 per cent citing having tanned skin.

Just one in five British women consider themselves attractive

Seventy-two per cent said being attractive made you popular, while more than half had regularly heard their mother complaining about her appearance.

The celebrities they would most like to look like are former S Club 7 and solo pop star Rachel Stevens and American singer Britney Spears.

Sylvia Lagnado, global brand director of Dove, said: 'We want more women to feel that beauty is within their reach and this study is instrumental in showing us how to achieve this goal.

'The results demonstrate the need to present a wider definition of beauty than is currently available to women – regardless of where they live.'

- This article first appeared in the *Daily Mail*, 3 January 2005.

© 2006 Associated Newspapers Ltd

Celebrities distort girls' search for ideal shape

Survey of teenagers reveals discontent with personal appearance and a preoccupation with the desire to acquire the perfect form

By Laura Barton

Just 8% of teenage girls in Britain deem themselves to be happy with their body, according to a body image survey commissioned by a teen magazine.

A further 68% believe their faces to be unattractive, and their lives are preoccupied by the desire to acquire a 'perfect' celebrity body.

Bliss magazine, which is aimed at girls aged 13 to 18, questioned 2,000 girls over 10 television regions, including Scotland, Wales and Northern Ireland. The average respondent was 14, 5ft 4in tall and weighed 8st 8lb (163cm and 54.4kg).

The survey found that while 58% of teenage girls believe themselves to be of normal weight – with 35% describing themselves as overweight and 7% underweight – 66% think they need to lose weight and 71% claim they would be '100% happier if they could lose half a stone'.

'We get a lot of letters from our readers about body image,' said Chantelle Horton, deputy editor of *Bliss*. 'There are letters about the extremes of obesity and anorexia, but in general body obsession is a defining factor.

'I think the female obsession with body image is not a new phenomenon, but young girls are now exposed to more images of "perfection" all the time – in magazines, on TV, in films and music videos and advertisements.'

The study also revealed some disquieting trends in teenage girls' eating habits. Just 48% said they eat vegetables every day, while precisely the same number said they ate chocolate on a daily basis.

A quarter of respondents admitted they had already suffered from an eating disorder – 6% citing anorexia, 5% bulimia and 14% binge-eating.

Ann McPherson, an Oxfordshire GP who treats teenagers with eating disorders, and runs the website teenagehealthfreak.org, was not surprised by the survey's findings.

'It's pretty awful, isn't it?' she said. 'There's pressure on young girls [to look a certain way] and there's pressure on women – it runs the whole way through. One would like girls to feel good about themselves and not feel they had to conform to stereotypes.'

> **66% of teenage girls think they need to lose weight and 71% claim they would be '100% happier if they could lose half a stone'**

The study found that 65% of girls had dieted in the past, with 14% describing themselves as constantly on a diet, and 32% saying they would consider plastic surgery.

'They don't think of long-term solutions to their body image problems,' says Horton. 'It's all about the quick fix – and that's drilled into them by the fact their mums might be on the Atkins diet or they see a celebrity with a wonky nose who gets it fixed with surgery.'

Images of 'perfect' celebrities were cited by 67% as a source of pressure to be slimmer. Similar numbers said they felt pressure from boys (65%) and other girls (63%).

Asked to nominate celebrities with the best bodies, the curvaceous J-Lo, Beyoncè and Britney Spears took the top three places.

Asked to construct the perfect female form, the teenagers plumped for Beyoncè's face, Jennifer Aniston's hair and arms, Christina Aguilera's breasts, Britney Spears's stomach, Jamelia's legs and J-Lo's derrière.

'J-Lo, Beyoncè, Britney ... none of them are stick insects,' Horton observed. 'They're all curvy and they've all spoken publicly about their physical flaws.'

Ultimately, however, it is teenage girls' relentless exposure to images of celebrities that may be distorting their body image.

Images of 'perfect' celebrities were cited by 67% as a source of pressure to be slimmer. Similar numbers said they felt pressure from boys (65%) and other girls (63%)

'Teenagers have always worried about their bodies,' said Dr McPherson, 'but I think now their worries are exacerbated with the whole promotion of the celebrity.'

'I think that dieting is just silly'

Alana Barlow, 15, of Manchester

I don't think I'm fat, I don't think I'm skinny. I hope I'm normal weight – I don't want to lose any weight. I like my height as well.

I'm not surprised by the survey, though. Sometimes I feel like that about my body, on a bad day, and I know a lot of friends who often feel that way.

I eat a lot of chocolate every day, but other than that I eat healthily and I do quite a lot of exercise – I walk a lot, do PE at school, and tae kwon do and kayaking.

I think dieting's silly and so does my mum. My friends aren't on diets, but a lot say they want to eat healthier. I think it's just a way of dieting, really.

The majority of girls at my school seem to feel happy with themselves, though I do know people who've made themselves sick.

I know girls who say they're too fat. But they don't do anything about it, just moan.

One girl I know went on a crash diet. She'd have a bowl of cereal for breakfast and say that was all she'd had to eat all day. She only kept it up three days.

Celebrities in general are too skinny – they're a bad example. Girls need a role-model who's positive about herself. Maybe like Pink.

J-Lo and Beyoncè – people say they're curvy but it's still a shape girls feel they have to look like. And that's not good.

5 January 2005

Plastic fantastic

Brits believe happiness is only a nip and tuck away

Happiness is only a surgeon's knife away, or so the results of a new study from Lloyds TSB Personal Lending would suggest. Six out of ten Brits (57 per cent) believe that going under the knife is the key to true happiness.

The study, which surveyed over 1,200 people across the UK, was undertaken by Lloyds TSB Personal Lending which has witnessed a dramatic increase in the popularity of bank loans for cosmetic surgery. A massive 90 per cent of the population would like to change something about the way they look and one in ten would consider a loan as a way to fund a nip and a tuck.

Tony Gibbons, director of Lloyds TSB Personal Lending, said, 'Figures from the British Association of Aesthetic Plastic Surgeons show cosmetic surgery operations rose by more than half last year. This comes as no surprise to us as plastic surgery has become a standard request for getting a loan up there with home improvements and buying a car. In the past we've logged loan requests for "plastic surgery" under miscellaneous but due to the increase we're looking to set up a dedicated "cosmetic surgery" category.

'While there's a mixture of people requesting money for medical reasons and self-improvement, "plastic surgery" is becoming less taboo and people aren't shy to admit that's what they want to spend their money on.'

Ninety-five per cent of those surveyed believe that looking better would also boost their confidence. However, the quest for happiness doesn't stop there, we'd also like to improve the way our partner looks! Eight per cent of women and 15 per cent of men would like their partner to have surgery.

When it comes to the image-conscious world of celebrity where the 'plastic fantastic' phenomenon is widespread, Anne Robinson is considered to have had the best surgery (33 per cent) followed closely by Liz Hurley (29 per cent). Jackie Stallone was judged to have the worst surgery securing a whopping 64 per cent of the vote, followed by Jordan (19 per cent), suggesting that celebrities can go too far in the quest for aesthetic perfection and ultimately happiness.

Notes

Research carried out by 72 Point during January 2005. 1,200 people were surveyed.

1 February 2005

■ The above information is reprinted with kind permission from Lloyds TSB. Visit www.lloydstsb.com for more information.

'My daughter wants surgery . . . she is 13'

Sarah Womack talks to a mother about her girls' obsession with image

Lisa Hogan, 37, a mother of four girls under 14, admits her daughters are influenced by celebrity magazines and television 'makeover' programmes to such an extent that they are already expressing a desire to lose weight and have plastic surgery.

As new research claims that girls as young as five are dissatisfied with their image, Lisa said her 13-year-old daughter Emily wants cosmetic surgery on her nose, eyes and thighs. She has wanted to lose weight since she was eight.

New research claims that girls as young as five are dissatisfied with their image

---

Together with two of her sisters, Hannah, aged 11, and Rachel, nine, Emily got out a tape measure and started measuring her hips when a would-be supermodel on Living TV's *America's Next Top Model* was told she was too fat.

'The model's hips were around 34 or 35 inches and it was suggested to this girl that she should not wear a certain gown because it made her look big,' said Lisa, from Bishop's Stortford, Herts. 'Emily got the tape measure and measured her hips and then of course the other two girls wanted to have a go.' The three girls also like *Extreme Makeover*, a TV series which departs from conventional makeover staples such as new clothes, make-up and hair, and offers participants plastic surgery ranging from tummy tucks and collagen injections to upper eye lifts and lip 'enhancement'. Its motto is: 'We'll stop at nothing to turn ordinary into extraordinary.'

'When Emily talks about losing weight or plastic surgery, my husband Sean and I tell her she looks absolutely fine as she is,' says Lisa. 'But she just replies: "You are biased because you are my parents."

'She is only a size eight to 10, and there is no fat on her at all. The other two girls are also on the skinny side, but Rachel has been called "fat" by a girl in her class.'

The UK Eating Disorders Association receives 20,000 telephone calls a year to its helpline from girls not dissimilar to Emily for whom the desire to lose weight has become an obsession, manifesting itself as an eating disorder.

The Association has received enquiries from children as young as eight, but says the peak age for problems such as anorexia nervosa, a life-threatening disorder characterised by a desire to lose large amounts of weight rapidly, and bulimia, an obsession to lose weight by ensuring that food is not allowed to stay in the body, is 14 to 18.

Steve Bloomfield, its spokesman, said that as a society 'we are perhaps becoming super-sensitive to the issue of obesity'.

Academics agree, saying the Government's anti-obesity campaign may be exacerbating the problem because it makes very young children overly conscious about their weight.

Dr Andrew Hill, a senior lecturer in behavioural sciences at Leeds University Medical School, said: 'Children are picking up on the anti-fat culture expounded by the media and health professionals at a very early age. Being fat was once an appearance issue. Now we are saying that being fat is bad for you.'

He pointed out that it was entirely normal for young children to put on weight at different stages in their physical development. 'In puberty, girls double in body fat. They are physically gaining the body tissue they need for fertility. Unless you have enough body fat, you won't menstruate.'

Younger children were teasing each other about having a fat bottom or legs when in fact what they were looking at was puppy fat, he said. These so-called fat youngsters would grow into adults of an average weight.

Deanne Jade, the founder of the National Centre for Eating Disorders, said the latest research did not surprise her. 'Our children are getting anxious younger and losing their innocence younger.' But she added that six-year-olds worrying about being thin 'won't necessarily lead to more eating disorders or to an epidemic of anorexia'. Anorexia tended to happen where people had a distorted image of their body, a specific type of dieting behaviour and nothing to compensate in their lives for their low self-esteem.

Many young people found compensation in having a sense of humour, plenty of friends or a talent.

8 March 2005

Boys and body image

One in four teenage boys think they may need cosmetic surgery

The obsession with body image has spread from girls to boys, according to research published today which says that eight in 10 teenage males are unhappy with their appearance.

A survey of 2,000 teenage boys, whose average age was 15, found that they are as self-conscious about their bodies as girls, with 62 per cent not liking their faces and 68 per cent not liking their teeth.

A quarter thought they may have cosmetic surgery and only four in 10 thought their fathers looked good for their age.

More than half of the boys questioned thought they were not attractive to girls, and eighty per cent said getting into physical shape would improve the quality of their life and make them happier. The boys in the survey said that they looked in the mirror on average 10 times a day.

The research follows academic reports, published in the *British Journal of Developmental Psychology*, showing that, in the age of the celebrity and makeovers, girls as young as five are unhappy with their bodies and want to be slimmer. But there has been little evidence so far to suggest that boys are as insecure as girls.

In this survey, David Beckham – the England football captain who has painted his nails, braided his hair and posed for gay magazines while maintaining a manly profile on the pitch – was the teenage boys' body and style icon.

But unlike Beckham, 69 per cent of the boys thought they looked their most appealing in jeans and T-shirt. Only 14 per cent thought they would look attractive to women in a suit.

Michelle Garnett, the editor of *Sneak* magazine, which undertook the research on boys by publishing a questionnaire and inviting teenagers to respond on the internet, said: 'Beckham is still the mainstream style icon, despite his unconventional clothes choice. The nail varnish and

By Sarah Womack, Social Affairs Correspondent

kaftans don't seem to have put boys off – they still think he looks cool. Boys are comparing themselves to celebrity male role models who are well known for their physiques and who trade on their good looks.

> *A survey of 2,000 teenage boys, whose average age was 15, found that they are as self-conscious about their bodies as girls, with 62 per cent not liking their faces and 68 per cent not liking their teeth*

'The boom in cosmetic surgery and the blanket coverage it receives has made it seem acceptable and desirable despite the fact that the role models of teenage boys have not had the procedures themselves.' Following in the footsteps of metrosexuals, 95 per cent of teenage boys think that good grooming improves their prospects with girls.

They spend an average of £24 a month on 'grooming products' and, the research claims, 72 per cent would like a makeover.

Of those teenage boys questioned, 96 per used deodorant, 90 per cent hair-styling products, 72 per cent aftershave and 50 per cent have tried moisturiser. Forty per cent claim to have used hand cream, and 17 per cent have used fake tanning products.

They say they spend 65 minutes getting ready for a night out and 34 minutes getting ready for school. A third think they need to lose weight and have tried to diet an average of four times.

Garnett said: 'When boys see masculine men like Gavin Henson, the rugby player, paying obvious attention to their appearance, taboos about fake tanning and beauty regimes are broken down. Suddenly, taking care of their bodies seems less "girlie" and embarrassing.'

Jack O'Sullivan, the co-founder of Fathers Direct, the national information service for fathers, said there was a culture of female affirmation, but 'we don't have a similar culture supporting men and masculinity.

'I support the affirmation of women but it sometimes feels like a put-down of men. And men's magazines parade men's vices rather than present aspirational views.

'So many magazine images are of the perfect man and what he is supposed to look like and it is ever harder for young men to measure up.'

24 May 2005

© *Telegraph Group Limited, London 2005*

Over 22,000 surgical procedures in 2005

British Association of Aesthetic Plastic Surgeons report 35% UK increase

BAAPS

The British Association of Aesthetic Plastic Surgeons (www.baaps.org.uk), the not-for-profit organisation established for the advancement of education and practice of Aesthetic Plastic Surgery for public benefit, today announced the results of their annual audit for 2005.

Highlights

- 22,041 surgical procedures were carried out by BAAPS members, up 34.6% from 2004.
- While the majority of cosmetic surgery continues to be carried out on women, the number of men having aesthetic procedures rose from 1,348 in 2004 to 2,440.
- From representing only 8% in 2004, men now account for 11% of the total procedures.
- Women had 19,601 procedures in 2005, up from 15,019 the previous year.
- The top procedure for women was breast augmentation, with 5,646 carried out – a 51% rise since 2004, when 3,731 were performed.

- Rhinoplasty continues to be the top procedure for men, with 735 undertaken by BAAPS members, up from 462 performed in 2004.
- Anti-ageing procedures (facelifts, eyelid surgery and brow lifts) showed a considerable rise in popularity in the last year, increasing by 42.1%, 50.2% and 34.8%, respectively.

According to Mr Adam Searle, consultant plastic surgeon and President of the BAAPS:

'These figures appear to represent a growing acceptance of aesthetic surgery, particularly in maintaining appearance with age and the number of men choosing to undergo surgery. With the increasing media coverage that provides the public with ever more information on what surgical procedures might achieve, it is essential that our members continue to promote sensible and responsible practices. At the BAAPS we are committed to educating people considering plastic surgery by providing independent and serious advice to assist in sensible decision-making.'

The figures in full

A total of 22,041 procedures were carried out this year by BAAPS members in their private practices, compared to 16,367 in 2004. 2005 results indicate that surgical numbers continue to grow, with a 34.6% rise over the previous year.

The top ten surgical procedures for men and women in 2005 were, in order of popularity:

- Breast augmentation: 5,655 – up 51.4% from last year
- Blepharoplasty (eyelids): 3,415 – up 50.2%
- Breast reduction: 2,700 – up 9.3%
- Face/neck lift: 2,279 – up 42.1%
- Rhinoplasty: 2,268 – up 34.7%
- Abdominoplasty: 1,869 – up 24.4%
- Liposuction (major): 1,436 – up 24.9%
- Otoplasty (ears): 1,176 – up 28.1%
- Liposuction (minor): 663 – up 9.6%
- Brow lifts 580 – up 34.8%.

Women had 89% of all cosmetic procedures (19,601, up from 15,019 in 2004). The top five surgical procedures for women in 2004 were: breast augmentation (5,646), blepharoplasty or eyelid surgery (2,868), breast reduction (2,593), face/neck lift (2,135), and rhinoplasty (1,533).

Men had 2,440 cosmetic procedures, an increase of 1,092 from 2004. The top five surgical procedures for

Rhinoplasty
Abdominoplasty
Otoplasty
Minor Liposuction
Major Liposuction

Breast augmentation
Breast reduction
Blepharopasty
Face/neck lift
Brow lift

men in 2005 were: rhinoplasty (735), blepharoplasty (547), otoplasty (526), liposuction (220), and face/neck lift (144).

According to Mr Douglas Mc-George, consultant plastic surgeon and President-Elect:

'These increases maintain a solid trend – evidently, the British public want to feel good about the way they look as they age. A growing awareness of the procedures available and their continued safety are all contributors to the popularity of cosmetic procedures. When performed under the right circumstances, aesthetic surgery can have a very positive psychological impact and improve a patient's quality of life.'

According to Mr Rajiv Grover, consultant plastic surgeon and BAAPS Council member responsible for the UK aesthetic surgery audit:

'I was not surprised at the continued rise in numbers, especially in the area of anti-ageing surgery such as eyelid surgery and facelifting. With these procedures it is essential to be selective in choosing the right practitioner, as the results are long lasting but complications can be permanent. Patients have come to view the BAAPS as the ideal destination to find out more about the possibilities and realities of aesthetic surgery.'
16 January 2006

■ The above information is reprinted with kind permission from the British Association of Aesthetic Plastic Surgeons. For more information, visit their website at www.baaps.org.uk.

© BAAPS

Children's body image

Now girls as young as five think they have to be slim to be popular

Girls as young as five are unhappy with their bodies and want to be thinner, according to a study which blames peer pressure in a child's early years at school.

Most girls thought that being slim would make them more popular, claimed the research in the *British Journal of Developmental Psychology*. They would also have no hesitation in dieting if they gained weight. The study was conducted among five- to eight-year-olds in South Australia, but experts said last night that British children felt 'paranoid' about their weight – partly because of the Government's anti-obesity message.

Most girls thought that being slim would make them more popular

Dr Andrew Hill, of Leeds University Medical School, said research among more than 200 eight-year-olds showed a high awareness of the campaign against obesity. 'Children have absorbed anti-fat messages loud and clear', he said. 'To get people to listen about a condition, you talk it up, and we have got obesity on the health agenda.'

'We have upped the ante, adding to negativity about being fat, but we

By Sarah Womack, Social Affairs Correspondent

need to be careful now so people are not paranoid about being fat.

'We want people who are overweight to do something about it. We don't want to terrorise youngsters.'

The UK Eating Disorders Association said it was known that children as young as eight had been diagnosed with eating disorders and there may have been instances in younger children.

A spokesman said: 'Low self-esteem is a major contributory factor of eating disorders: media images, peer pressure and family situations can also affect people. We are concerned but not surprised that school children as young as six are affected by them.'

The latest research was conducted by academics at Flinders University among 81 girls. They were asked what they thought about their peers' level of unhappiness with their bodies and if they discussed body shape.

Almost half (46.9 per cent) wanted to be thinner, and 45.7 per cent said they would go on a diet if they gained weight. Among five-year-olds, 28.6 per cent wished they were thinner. After being shown pictures of a girl before and after putting on weight, 35 per cent of the girls thought her eating habits were to blame, and 28.6 per cent said she should go on a diet. Around 71 per cent of girls aged seven said they wanted to be thinner.

The report's authors said: 'Body dissatisfaction and dieting awareness develop over the first two years of schooling.'

Most of the girls believed that being thin would make them more likeable, although few said they discussed their bodies with friends. Their ideas about their friends' unhappiness with their bodies were linked to their own unhappiness with their bodies.

'It is therefore possible that peer transmissions of ideals about appearance could also occur through comments when trying on clothes or talking about pop stars when watching television,' the report said.

Deanne Jade, of the National Centre for Eating Disorders, said the research should be treated cautiously because children often picked out a thin image as desirable when shown one by researchers but had no problem making friends with children of all shapes and sizes at school.

'What we do know, however, is that by the time they reach adulthood, 95 per cent of women are dissatisfied with their bodies and seven out of 10 girls have been on a diet,' she said.
8 March 2005
© *Telegraph Group Limited, London 2005*

Little miss perfect

With schoolgirls opting for breast enlargements and nose jobs, and parents readily agreeing to (and paying for) the operations, has the craze for plastic surgery finally gone too far? Sarah Ebner meets three teenagers who claim a scalpel changed their lives

Aimee Cookson is standing in front of a mirror that hangs in her bedroom. Wearing jeans and a tight top and surrounded by photographs of her friends, she looks like a typical, fashion-conscious teenager. Except, that is, for her fake breasts.

'Kids at school used to call me "Pancake", or even "Holland",' says Aimee in her strong Mancunian accent. 'I was always small. I wore padded bras and felt like a little girl next to my mates. I was only just a 34A, now I'm a big C and feel a lot better.' Aimee, who decided to have breast implants when she was only 16, finally went under the surgeon's knife in May last year – two months after her 18th birthday.

Her boyfriend was all in favour of the surgery and her grandmother, with whom she lives, gave her £2,000 towards the £4,000 cost of the operation. 'It was a lot of money,' admits Aimee. 'I thought, "I could get a really nice car for that." But then I thought, "I could get my breasts done and buy a cheap car instead."'

Aimee's tale illustrates a growing trend. Not satisfied with the transforming effects of make-up, clothes or hairstyles, more young women are turning to surgery to 'correct' the bodies with which they were born. Transform Medical Group – the largest private cosmetic surgery provider in Britain – says there has been a ten per cent increase in the number of women in their teens and early twenties having surgery in the last year. The most popular procedure is breast enlargement, but others beg their parents to pin back their ears or make their noses smaller.

It's all part of an industry valued at more than £250 million a year. For her part, Aimee says she is delighted with her new breasts and is now considering a career in modelling. 'I'm definitely happier,' she says. 'It was the right thing for me. There are people who aren't attractive and want to look better. I don't see why they shouldn't have that chance.'

Dr Eileen Bradbury, a psychologist based at the Alexandra Hospital in Cheshire, disagrees. She says many teenagers now regard surgery as a quick cure-all and turn to a plastic surgeon instead of seeking long-term solutions for problems such as low self-esteem, eating disorders, loneliness and bullying. 'Young people are under pressure to look good all the time,' says Bradbury, who assesses and counsels people before and after plastic surgery.

> *'Plastic surgery is led by the cult of celebrity, and people think there's a kind of magic to it. Often they don't even see it as a medical procedure'*

'There have been increases in anorexia and other eating disorders in recent years, and I think the same forces and pressures are at play here – a sense that you have to be thin and you have to be beautiful. The period between 18 and 20 is a fragile time, which can be quite scary. Everyone around you can seem confident and look good, and you never know if they actually feel like you do. It's an age where really you have to ask yourself some hard questions, and the crucial one is, "What do you expect to be different in your life because of surgery?" It's buying into a false belief to think your life will be better if you have it.'

But many people – young and old – do buy into that belief, which is not surprising, considering the number of television shows and magazine articles that venerate the powers of the cosmetic surgeon. 'I've worked in plastic surgery units for two decades,' says Bradbury, 'and I've seen it change from something highly secretive to

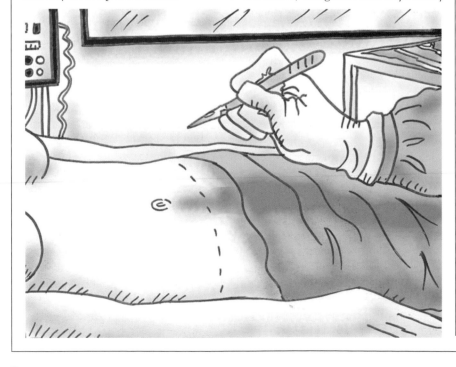

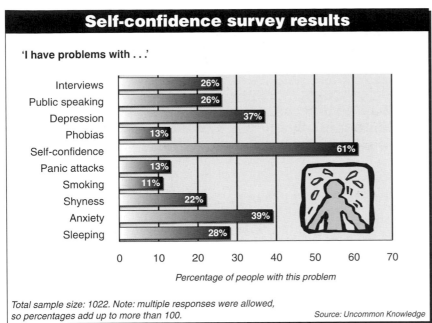

Self-confidence survey results

'I have problems with . . .'

Problem	Percentage of people with this problem
Interviews	26%
Public speaking	26%
Depression	37%
Phobias	13%
Self-confidence	61%
Panic attacks	13%
Smoking	11%
Shyness	22%
Anxiety	39%
Sleeping	28%

Percentage of people with this problem (scale 0–70)

Total sample size: 1022. Note: multiple responses were allowed, so percentages add up to more than 100.

Source: Uncommon Knowledge

something normal which everyone talks about. It's led by the cult of celebrity, and people think there's a kind of magic to it. Often they don't even see it as a medical procedure or worry about it going wrong.'

Certainly, Aimee has no qualms about her operation. She knew there were dangers and was prepared for the discomfort. 'It was bearable,' she says. 'And definitely worth it.' And it hasn't put her off the idea of messing about with other parts of her body. 'If I had the money, I'd get more done.' It's that kind of cavalier attitude that concerns some plastic surgeons.

Jagdeep Chana, a consultant who works for the NHS at the Mount Vernon Hospital in Middlesex, and privately in Hertfordshire, worries that younger girls need to be carefully counselled before surgery. He's critical of the hard-sell tactics employed by large organisations that advertise in women's magazines, and also of reality-television programmes such as *Extreme Makeover* and *The Swan*.

'A half-hour television programme is like a snapshot,' he says. 'It tends to give the impression that everything went quickly and smoothly and is now fine and great. People are shocked when I say there's a four to six week recovery time. They are given unrealistic expectations.

'If you're under 20, you may not be mature enough to appreciate all the implications,' adds Chana. 'I get girls coming to see me because they want breast augmentation, but they don't realise it's a lifelong commitment. They need to think years down the line, particularly financially. Implants have to be replaced after ten to 15 years, and the shape of breasts may change with age and following pregnancy, too.'

There are many reasons why people have plastic surgery. Sometimes it's to stand out – to look more attractive than the norm or to have bigger breasts – but with teenagers it's quite often the opposite, to fit in better, and be one of the girls. That was the motivation of 18-year-old Kayleigh Wallace. She had a rhinoplasty (nose operation) four months ago, and says it has done wonders for her self-esteem. 'I just wanted to like myself more,' she says. 'I didn't like the way I looked and thought people would like me more if I looked better.' Kayleigh, who lives with her mother in Hemel Hempstead, Hertfordshire, is tiny and slim, with blonde hair and huge blue eyes.

Despite her new nose (which looks neutral – not too big or too

small) she still seems extraordinarily shy and withdrawn, something she blames on her (old) nose. Haltingly, Kayleigh explains that she was bullied at school and told her nose was 'big and horrible'. She clearly went through a difficult time and is keen to demonstrate just how bad her old nose was. 'You can't really see the lump properly on that,' she says earnestly, holding up a photograph of herself before surgery. She handles it gingerly, as if it's something distasteful, but, to be honest, it doesn't look that bad to me.

Even so, her mother Linda believes the operation, which she fully supported and for which she paid almost £4,000, was well worth it. 'Before, it was like a big nose on a little face. I felt guilty because it came from my side of the family,' she says. 'Kayleigh kept going on at me to do "something" about it, and although she only had the operation in October, it's made such a difference. She was really depressed – now she holds her head up.'

'A half-hour television programme is like a snapshot. It tends to give the impression that everything went quickly and smoothly and is now fine and great'

Aimee Cookson didn't have such an easy time convincing her grandmother, Sandy Moore, that surgery was necessary. 'She had no bust at all,' says Sandy. 'She felt so conscious of not being able to wear a top without a padded bra, and now she's much more confident. I said that it wasn't important, that it didn't matter. But she thought differently.'

Surely, though, if Sandy hadn't relented and given Aimee the money, she would have had no choice but to wait. 'She was so determined to do it that even when I said no, she told me she would get a loan,' Sandy counters. 'I could just imagine the kind of interest a loan company would charge. I wasn't going to let her get into that sort of debt. Aimee's not spoilt. She doesn't get everything she wants and I certainly wouldn't have just given her the money for this. She has to pay me back.'

Like Aimee, Caroline Berry, a bright, attractive and vivacious 19-year-old from Kent, had to fight to persuade her parents that surgery was absolutely necessary. But she, too, eventually prevailed. Earlier this year her parents took out a £6,000 loan to pay for an operation to make her breasts more symmetrical. 'With my clothes on, you can't really see a difference to how I looked before,' says Caroline. 'But I had developed in a funny way and it was obvious with my clothes off. I called them my orang-utan boobs – both drooped and were a lot lower than they should have been. It was something I was always aware of. For a 19-year-old, they were below par.'

Caroline, who appears to be level-headed enough, is keen to emphasise that she did not want bigger breasts, but balanced ones. The fact that her surgeon also put in implants is, she suggests breezily, an added extra which she thought she may as well go for. But Caroline, like Aimee and Kayleigh, does not work, and could not afford to pay for surgery herself. She intended to pay back the loan her parents took out, but has since gone back to college and has no money to do so.

'I do feel guilty,' she says. 'It's hard. But I don't take, take, take all the time. I dress in clothes from Primark, and I do buy my mum flowers.' And what about her parents? Do they regret their decision? Mrs Berry admits she was concerned about her daughter having surgery, and thought she 'looked lovely as she was'. However, she says that Caroline's unhappiness persuaded her it was the right thing to do.

'If you're unhappy and there's a way of doing something about it, why not?'

'She was very, very unhappy. As she got older, having this done became more and more important to her. It was something very personal to her and she really wanted it. I think that if you can, you've got to go with trying to make your daughter happy. We're lucky that we could do it.'

Peter Arnstein, Caroline's surgeon and one of the 'stars' of the television show *Extreme Makeover UK*, welcomes such instances of parental support, but believes teenagers are old enough to make up their own minds. 'Parents are involved and that can only be a good thing,' he says. 'In any case, young people nowadays are incredibly information-literate, and when they come to see me it's usually easy to tell why they want something done. They may have a degree of asymmetry, or small breasts, and I don't see it as a moral issue. As long as a patient is entirely aware, who are we to judge them on their aspirations?'

Arnstein says he would have few qualms about operating on his own 17-year-old daughter, if she so desired, or indeed on someone even younger. 'Why should someone have to wait until they're in their twenties to have something done, when they already feel deformed?' he asks. 'I would consider every case on its merits. People have always wanted to look better, and although surgery is more invasive than traditional ways of looking good, it isn't that much of a change. We're in a different world now and can't make things stand still. Just because it's new doesn?t make it bad.'

Arnstein says it's his duty to explain procedures and make sure his patients know about the risks. But he is adamant that surgery is not being used to 'sort out' different problems. 'It's the other way round,' he says. 'They want bigger breasts and that's it. Then it gives them more confidence. They're not doing it for a laugh, but for a particular reason.'

Aimee, Kayleigh and Caroline have no regrets. But for two of them, it is not the end of the story. As Aimee and Caroline get older, their implants will need to be replaced, meaning more operations and further cost.

'I'm not worried about other operations,' says Caroline. 'If I can get through the first one, I can certainly get through the second and third and fourth. I admit I'm young, but I don't think I should have waited. If you're unhappy and there's a way of doing something about it, why not?'

15 January 2006

© *Telegraph Group Limited, London 2006*

Ethnicity and body image

How much do your culture and ethnicity affect your body image? TheSite finds out

Positive body image

Research has shown that Black women with high self-esteem and a strong sense of racial identity actually rated themselves more attractive than pictures of supposedly 'beautiful' White fashion models. Other studies indicate that this may be because Western Black women are more flexible in their concepts of beauty than their White counterparts.

A British study showed that Asian-British women were more content with their body size than White British women, despite the fact that the Asians' ideal body size was as slim as that of the White women. This suggests that the Asian-British women were less concerned about matching the ideal than the White women. A study of Mexican immigrants in America found that those who had immigrated after the age of 17 were less affected by the super-thin ideal than those who were 16 or younger when they came to the US.

TheSite.org

Where things are changing

Root (1990) states that Black and Asian women who look and dress more like White women will have better jobs, salaries and social lives open to them than those who do not. Root feels this may put pressure on those with less Western looks to try and shape their bodies to fit the mainstream culture's female body ideal.

There is some evidence to support this. The thin ideal for women seems to be spreading across all ethnic groups. In the last ten years there has been a significant amount of dieting and body shaping among African American celebrities.

Performers such as Janet Jackson, Toni Braxton, and Oprah Winfrey have all become thin. Black female stars in the film, music and fashion industry are now just as thin as their White counterparts. And it is not just the UK and America where these changes are occurring. In traditional South African culture, a large posterior was favoured because it implied a woman was well looked after. But in recent years cosmetic surgery has come into vogue among up-and-coming black professionals.

A British study showed that Asian-British women were more content with their body size than White British women, despite the Asians' ideal body size being as slim as that of the White women

---

Cosmetic surgery

The desire to change how we look, not only through the colour of our skin, but with the shape of our bodies, highlights a world where many of us are still not comfortable in embracing our ethnicity. Ethnic minorities including Hispanics, Asians, and African Americans, are increasingly going under the knife.

- The US was one of the first countries to start the trend of creating bigger lips through botox lip-enhancing treatments. Women are even abandoning the waif look to get curves and a bootie like J-Lo through implants in their buttocks.
- Asian men and women have been going under the knife for eyelid surgery to make their eyes look more westernised and African Americans are slimming their noses down with rhinoplasty.

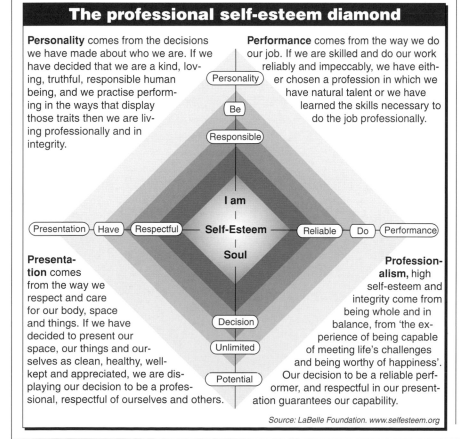

The professional self-esteem diamond

Personality comes from the decisions we have made about who we are. If we have decided that we are a kind, loving, truthful, responsible human being, and we practise performing in the ways that display those traits then we are living professionally and in integrity.

Performance comes from the way we do our job. If we are skilled and do our work reliably and impeccably, we have either chosen a profession in which we have natural talent or we have learned the skills necessary to do the job professionally.

Personality — Be — Responsible — I am — Self-Esteem — Soul — Decision — Unlimited — Potential

Presentation — Have — Respectful — Reliable — Do — Performance

Presentation comes from the way we respect and care for our body, space and things. If we have decided to present our space, our things and ourselves as clean, healthy, well-kept and appreciated, we are displaying our decision to be a professional, respectful of ourselves and others.

Professionalism, high self-esteem and integrity come from being whole and in balance, from 'the experience of being capable of meeting life's challenges and being worthy of happiness'. Our decision to be a reliable performer, and respectful in our presentation guarantees our capability.

Source: LaBelle Foundation. www.selfesteem.org

Danger zone

Any cosmetic surgery carries risks, but many people find that once they have changed one thing, it can become an addiction and there are other things they want altered.

The desire to change how we look, not only through the colour of our skin, but with the shape of our bodies, highlights a world where many of us are still not comfortable in embracing our ethnicity

---

Where things remain the same

- In Cameroon and many other parts of Africa, obesity, especially in the buttocks, has been associated with abundance, erotic desirability, and fertility. Fat has been seen as a statement of well-being and has been frequently produced artificially through fattening processes.
- In Jamaica, generally females want to be big; size 10 is too thin, while being a size 16 or above is seen as much more attractive. Weight is generally associated with wealth and prosperity and social status. So, instead of the health risks of crash diets, there is a new problem, that of fowl pills. These pills are simply hormone tablets used by farmers to fatten up hens before slaughter. They are being bought for just under a tenner a dozen by women desperate to get the perfect fuller figure. These pills contain the sex hormones, testosterone and progestogen, large doses of which can encourage breast cancer.

- Information reprinted with kind permission from TheSite. org. Visit www.thesite.org for more information.

© *TheSite.org*

Healthy self-esteem

Information from Shining Bright

Our self-belief – and therefore our self-esteem – is based around how we think, feel and behave. The following are examples of thoughts, feelings and behaviour which suggest a healthy level of self-esteem and a balanced approach to life.

People who have healthy self-esteem tend to:

Thoughts

- Be able to believe themselves
- Think that they deserve the best in life
- Think they are worthy
- Respect themselves and others
- Are successful and try to be the best they can be
- Be able to change or 'make things happen'.

Feelings

- Like themselves and are able to laugh at themselves
- Be relaxed and confident (without appearing to be overbearing)
- Be able to take criticism on board
- Be able to forgive mistakes made by self and others
- Have a balanced and positive approach to life
- Feel motivated with a clear sense of direction
- Feel secure and not overly worried about what others think.

Behaviour

- Be decisive and are able to confidently view options
- Exude a sense of well-being
- Communicate in an open way
- Not be overly critical of themselves or others
- Be resourceful and self-reliant but able to ask for help if required
- Be able to honour their achievements and successes
- Be able to take risks
- Be able to say 'no'
- Be able to show their feelings and emotions openly.

Positive Effects

People with healthy self-esteem tend to be motivated and positive. They feel able to take risks and effectively change aspects of their life and behaviour. They tend to be successful and happy and feel worthy and secure. Does this sound like you? Or does this sound like the you you would like to be?

- The above information is reprinted with kind permission from Shining Bright. Visit www.shining-bright.co.uk for more information.

© *Shining Bright*

How to increase your self-esteem

Information from Mind

**For better
mental health**

'It's a funny thing… when I was involved in a wider political struggle, when it was a question of standing up for human rights in general, on behalf of other people, I could keep going, I could even face prison. But when it comes to sorting out a problem like being charged too much council tax, I just go to pieces inside and have to leave it all to my wife.'

'Now that I'm all on my own, I don't bother to prepare proper meals. There doesn't seem much point when it's only me.'

'When I stop doing things and just pause, I feel quite empty.'

'None of my colleagues remembered my birthday… but then, what can you expect in a place like this?'

These are quotations from people with low self-esteem. This article is for anyone who wants to help themselves or others to deal with the feelings and experiences that undermine them. It explains how to recognise the problem, and what you can do to improve it.

What is self-esteem?

When your self-esteem is low, you feel depressed and hopeless. You see life negatively. Everything seems difficult, or too much trouble. It feels as if the world is a bad place, full of people who will abuse or ignore you, and you feel unable to do anything about it. You see yourself as a victim. You treat other people as potential enemies, or saviours, and sooner or later they treat you badly or let you down. This sets up a vicious circle.

When your self-esteem is high, on the other hand, the world feels like a good place, full of friends, potential pleasures and opportunities. You can assert yourself, ask for what you want and express your feelings. You

feel potent, and know that you can make a difference. Other people, in general, respond to your positive attitude, so that, even when you don't get your way, you feel good about yourself and them. This reinforces your self-esteem and stimulates your inner growth.

What we've described are the two ends of a spectrum. If they were shown as two points joined by a line, few of us would say that we live at either end of it. Most of us get through life somewhere near the positive end, and we move up and down it in response to things that happen to us. Events involving loss or threat, such as losing your job, ending a relationship, being bereaved, falling ill or having your house broken into, can give your self-esteem a huge knock. On the other hand, when you are promoted, fall in love, pass an exam, face a challenge or win a prize, then you feel pleased and proud; your self-esteem is boosted. A healthy person can absorb most knocks to their self-esteem and bounce back, if their basic sense of self is positive.

Some people don't have a positive sense of self, however. It's as if their most comfortable postion on this spectrum (the one that they always tend to return to) is at the negative end. When they get a knock, they can't bounce back. They are suffering from chronic low self-esteem.

What causes low self-esteem?

If you lose your job after several years of calm and happy employment, when your family life is going well, it may be devastating, initially, but once the shock has worn off you have a good chance of finding the resources to cope. If, on the other hand, you have just been divorced and have moved house when you receive your redundancy notice, and then hear the next day that a parent has terminal cancer, then recovery is bound to be much more difficult. Sometimes life just throws an unbearable amount of trouble at us, all at once, and we have to mobilise all the support we can from friends, family and community to help us survive it.

Problems left over from childhood

We may be vulnerable because of unsorted childhood issues. Heavy blows dealt to our self-esteem early in life can undermine our capacity to respond positively to the challenges we face later on, as adults, if we have not had the chance to address or to heal them. (See below for more information.)

Physical ill-health

Our self-esteem is bound up with our physical wellbeing, and is vulnerable to illness and injury. If we get ill or have an accident, it can feel as if our body has betrayed us. Our trust in the world as a safe place may be shaken, temporarily. If the illness or accident involves us in a spell in hospital, it can further damage our self-esteem.

A sense of powerlessness

The more we feel potent, the better our self-esteem. Redundancy may not feel so bad if you think you can easily get another job, even a better one; if not, it can feel devastating. It can also feel devastating if you are the only one of a racial or social minority, and have reason to believe that you are the victim of prejudice. The degree of power you have depends not just on who you are, but also on where you are; in other words, on the social context. If you are not sure of your ground in any sense (for example because you are in a foreign culture, speaking an unfamiliar language, or in an unfamiliar role) you will feel disempowered. Institutions can increase or diminish the self-esteem of the people in them by their day-to-day practices. For example, some hospitals attach a plastic bracelet with a number on it to the patient's wrist, on admission. However necessary this may be, if you are the patient, it can feel as though the hospital is claiming your body as theirs, taking away a degree of power from you just when you most need it. On the other hand, if you are greeted with courtesy, treated with respect and given choices, this will enhance your self-esteem.

How does childhood experience affect self-esteem?

Children tend not to have much power or status in our society, and therefore may still be subject to many common experiences that can undermine their self-esteem. These include, in particular, violence, loss and neglect.

Domestic violence

A child may experience violence in many ways, all of them damaging. They may be subjected to corporal punishment, where a parent or other adult deliberately inflicts pain on them and does not allow them to fight back. Or they may witness domestic violence between their parents. Or they may be subjected to violence from a sibling or from another family member, which the parents fail to see or prevent. The violence does not have to be dramatic to be damaging. Indeed, dramatic violence that happens over a short period may attract attention and lead to changes in the family situation that will remedy it. Undercover violence that goes on for a long time, bullying by an older brother or sister for example, can be just as harmful.

Dealing with prejudice

Another form of violence is institutional prejudice, such as racism. A child may see a much-loved parent insulted, spat at or assaulted in the street, or doing work well below his or her capacity. He or she may come to realise that 'people like us' get the worst housing, and medical care. Or he or she may hear, in the media, insulting portrayals of groups that he or she identifies with. These amount to an attack on that child's self-esteem.

Facing loss

The death of a family member, such as a grandparent, or the sickness of a mother (especially if she has to go away to hospital or a convalescent home) are obvious examples of loss that can affect a small child. But more ordinary events, such as moving house, the birth of a new sibling, or the death of a loved pet, can all be experienced as devastating losses by a child. As such, they have to be acknowledged and mourned.

Emotional neglect

When we think of a neglected child, the image that comes to mind is often of fairly dramatic physical neglect, with the child unwashed, unfed, and left to roam the streets after dark at a young age. Yet there can be quite subtle emotional neglect, too, that can also be harmful. There are many things even loving and well-meaning parents can do that act against their children's need to feel loved and wanted:

- Leaving very small babies alone for hours at a time, to cry themselves to sleep. The more often, and the more lovingly, a baby is touched in its very early life, the more self-esteem he or she will have as an adult. The practice of baby massage would do wonders for the self-esteem of the next generation!
- Preferring one child over others (the only boy over his four sisters, or the youngest girl over the older children). This can happen without the parents realising they are doing it.
- Insisting that their child become what or who the parents want him or her to be, in spite of the child's natural talents and personality. Insisting, for instance, the child learn music when he would rather play football, or vice versa. Refusing to allow a daughter to take up engineering, or a son to study music because the parents think he should go into the family business.
- Not noticing the child's emotional needs. For instance, when he or she is mourning for a pet, reacting to the birth of a sibling, or having difficulties in settling in a new school.
- Discussing decisions that involve the child (about holidays or schooling) in front of the child, but without including him or her.
- Behaving, generally, as though the child's feelings and perceptions don't matter: 'You're too young to be thinking about that', 'Just shut up and do what you're told!'
- Not anwering, or refusing to discuss with the child important questions such as, 'Now Daddy's got this new job, are we going to move to Manchester?'
- Inconsistent discipline and expectations; blowing hot and cold with affection and attention.
- Blaming them for things over which they have no control.
- Exposing them to inappropriate sexual innuendo or activity.

With all this violence, loss and neglect what matters is not so much what happens to the child, as how the child is helped to make sense of the experience. A child needs to be comforted and given the chance to talk things over and to come to terms with it. If events can't be talked about and are buried, this will do far more harm to the child's self-esteem.

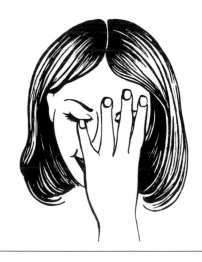

What can I do to heal the past?

Even if we had to bury a childhood hurt, such as neglect or violence, at the time, we can still find healing for it in adult life. The basic process is the same: to find a way of telling the story, to make sense of it, to be comforted, and to digest it all. An obvious way to do this is through therapy or counselling, but that may not be available or appropriate for everyone. Other ways include:

Children tend not to have much power or status in our society, and therefore may still be subject to many common experiences that can undermine their self-esteem. These include, in particular, violence, loss and neglect

---

- Through the expressive arts, such as dance, music, sculpting, painting, creative writing and poetry. All of these can help you to tell your story, and can give tremendous pleasure and empowerment in themselves. Find a class through your local adult education service, local library or community centre.

- Learn to be assertive. Read up on it, and join a class. It's also worth looking online for details of classes.

- Form a support group. Perhaps you can find others seeking help with their past, through a local community centre, bookshop, religious organisation or adult education class (on assertiveness or self-esteem, for example).

- Tell your friends that you are attempting to face some old childhood wounds, and enlist their help. They may have had similar experiences, and have useful advice and suggestions.

- Keep a journal. Use it to explore your memories and relate them to difficulties you are having now.

How can I build up my self-esteem?

Take care of your physical health

Make sure you have good food, relaxation and enough sleep. Try to do 10-15 minutes of moderate exercise (such as brisk walking) every day, and about 20 minutes of more vigorous exercise three times a week (something that raises your heartbeat and makes you sweat).

Have a massage whenever you can

Nothing is better for increasing self-esteem and beating stress! Learn to recognise your own stress indicators, and when they occur, take time out to look after yourself.

Reduce your stress levels

Whenever possible, avoid situations where you have little power, and institutions that undermine your self-esteem. This may be difficult or appear impossible in the short run, but may be essential to your long-term mental and physical wellbeing. Keep your home as stress free as possible: make sure it is as tidy as suits you, with good lighting and supportive seating.

Accepting a challenge

Set yourself a challenge that you can realistically achieve, and then go for it! Start with something relatively small, such as, 'Getting fit enough to walk up the steps to my flat without getting out of breath or taking the lift'. (But not 'Running the Marathon this year' unless, of course, that is a realistic goal for you!) Then, when you have achieved it, reward yourself! Tell your friends, and let them praise you for it. Then set yourself another challenge. Learn to enjoy your own achievements.

Learn something new

It doesn't really matter what it is, whether it's car maintenance, speaking Russian or flower arranging. The important thing is that it interests you and will give you a sense of achievement. The longer you have been away from learning anything new, and the more different the new subject is from your normal life, the more benefit this will give you. For example, if you are an intellectual sort of person, take up weight training or yoga. If you are a handy,

craftsmanlike person, try and learn a foreign language, or teach yourself a new style of dance.

Enjoying yourself

Find out what you most enjoy, and then find a way of doing it as much as possible. If you enjoy it, you probably have some talent for it, whatever it is. Doing what we are best at is the most empowering and self-nourishing kind of activity. (If your response to this advice is, 'But I'm not good at anything!', go back to the question, What can I do to heal the past?)

Taking action

Join in with others, if possible, to take action about the things that annoy you, whether it's the amount of dog mess in your street, Government policy on asylum-seekers, the worldwide arms trade, or whatever most angers you. Of course, the trick here is to find the right group of fellow-campaigners, a group where you feel respected and empowered. Unfortunately, political campaigning groups can be as damaging to the self-esteem of their members as any other kind of institutions! This is perhaps an area where continuing struggle is not only necessary, but a sign of love for oneself, one's fellow-humans and for the world, in general.

Giving yourself a treat

Give yourself regular treats, to remind yourself that you deserve nurture and pleasure. Programme some fun into your plans for each week, to bolster your sense of humour and creativity.

Making music

Learn to sing! To free your voice is empowering to mind, soul and body. Singing strengthens the lungs and the legs, gives joy and hope, and is a powerful medium for self-expression. You can do it alone, or as part of a group. Many places now have 'Choirs for the Tone Deaf' or 'Can't Sing' groups, which take on the fact that many of us may have had painful experiences with music teachers in the past. They can teach ways of addressing this, involving breath and relaxation techniques.

- The above information is reprinted with kind permission from Mind. Visit www.mind.org.uk for more information.

© Mind

Kick the habit of self-criticism

How often do you criticise yourself? Research shows that up to 90 per cent of people's thoughts are critical or judgmental. And the vast majority of these are aimed at oneself. Here's how to be kinder to yourself and boost your confidence

By Caro Handley

Critical behaviour has its origins in childhood. Most children are told something negative about themselves, far more often than they hear something positive. As they grow older they simply carry on with this pattern – they've no idea how to do it any other way. As adults, most of us have a mental tape which we play many times a day, 'I'm not good enough, I didn't do well enough, I don't deserve anything good' – or a variation on these themes. And of course we bring it into our working lives, where it makes enjoying your job and being good at it a whole lot harder.

> *Most of us have a mental tape which we play many times a day, 'I'm not good enough, I didn't do well enough, I don't deserve anything good'*

The good news is that once you realise you're doing this, you have the choice whether to carry on. Think about a friend you really value. If she, or he, felt they'd got something wrong or weren't good enough, you'd be quick to reassure them. So why treat yourself any differently? A best friend would do these things for you, but you can go one better and do them for yourself – in other words, be your own best friend.

Here's how:

1. Praise, praise, praise

For yourself, of course. Behaviourists now know that, with enough praise, even an appallingly behaved child can be quickly turned into a well-behaved little darling. And there's always something to praise, in everyone. You're in the best position to know how hard you work, how well you do, how many things you succeed in and how much you care. So pile on the praise.

2. Use affirmations

These are positive statements and have been proven to be powerfully effective in changing attitudes and behaviour. They must always be in the present tense, as though they were already true. For instance: 'I'm great at my job', 'I get noticed and appreciated at work', 'I love what I do, and succeed easily'. Come up with your own, write them down and put them somewhere prominent.

3. Repeat, repeat, repeat

Affirmations and positive self-talk need to be repeated as often as possible. That way, it really goes in, and it leaves less room for the negative stuff. Think of how many times during the day you remember something upsetting, for instance a rude comment by someone at work, or a job you think you did badly. Yes, hundreds. Well that's how often you've got to start remembering the good things about yourself.

4. Notice the good stuff

Because, we usually don't. We're too busy focusing on the one awful thing that happened in the day to notice the kind comment from a workmate or the praise we got from the boss. Notice them now, replay them to yourself often, write them down and put them in a 'wonderful me' box, tin or envelope. Sounds cheesy, but it you go back once a week and read them all, you'll glow!

■ The above information is reprinted with kind permission from iVillage. Visit www.ivillage.co.uk for more information.

© iVillage

7 ways to boost your self-esteem quickly

Low self-esteem can trip you up just when you need your self-esteem to be at its best. These 7 tips will help you feel better about yourself quickly

1) Think back to when you did something new for the first time

Learning something new is often accompanied by feelings of nervousness, lack of self-belief and high stress levels, all of which are necessary parts of the learning process. The next time you feel under-confident, remembering this will remind you that it's perfectly normal – you're just learning!

2) Do something you have been putting off

Like writing or calling a friend, cleaning the house, tidying the garden, fixing the car, organising the bills, making a tasty and healthy meal – anything that involved you making a decision, then following through!

3) Do something you are good at

Examples? How about swimming, running, dancing, cooking, gardening, climbing, painting, writing? If possible, it should be something that holds your attention and requires enough focus to get you into that state of 'flow' where you forget about everything else. You will feel more competent, accomplished and capable afterwards, great antidotes to low self-esteem!

And while you're at it, seriously consider doing something like this at least once a week. People who experience 'flow' regularly seem to be happier and healthier.

4) Stop thinking about yourself!

I know this sounds strange, but low self-esteem is often accompanied by too much focus on the self. Doing something that absorbs you and holds your attention can quickly make you feel better.

5) Get seriously relaxed

If you are feeling low, anxious or lacking in confidence, the first thing to do is to stop thinking and relax properly. Some people

do this by exercising, others by involving themselves in something that occupies their mind. However, being able to relax yourself when you want is a fantastic life skill and so practising self hypnosis, meditation, or a physically based relaxation technique such as Tai Chi can be incredibly useful.

> *For most people, good self-esteem is not just a happy accident, it's a result of the way they think and the things they do from day to day*

When you are properly relaxed, your brain is less emotional and your memory for good events works better. A great 'rescue remedy'!

6) Remember all the things you have achieved

This can be difficult at first, but after a while, you'll develop a handy mental list of self-esteem-boosting memories. And if you're thinking 'But I've never achieved anything', I'm not talking about climbing Everest here.

Things like passing your driving test (despite being nervous), passing exams (despite doubting that you

would), playing team sport, getting fit (even if you let it slip later), saving money for something, trying to help someone (even if it didn't work) and so on.

7) Remember that you could be wrong!

If you are feeling bad about yourself, remember that way you feel affects your thoughts, memory and behaviour. So when you feel bad, you will only remember the bad times, and will tend to be pessimistic about yourself. This is where the tip 'Get Seriously Relaxed' comes in!

Summary

Once you have tried out a few of these, consider making them a permanent part of your life. For most people, good self-esteem is not just a happy accident, it's a result of the way they think and the things they do from day to day. Good luck!

■ The above information is re-printed with kind permission from Uncommon Knowledge Ltd. Visit www.self-confidence.co.uk for more information.

© Uncommon Knowledge Ltd

Ten ways to boost your self-esteem

Hands up if you suffer from a lack of self-confidence. Well, that pretty much covers everyone. So what can you do about it? Quite a lot, says life coach Judith Verity

If you aren't happy with your life at the moment, don't worry, because you have the power to change it. It might not feel like it right now, but even small changes can make a very big difference.

If you don't think you can manage all ten of these confidence-boosting ideas straight away, just choose one and, when you've got the hang of it, do another one. In fact, you could even set yourself a two-week change programme and take one of the options each day.

1. De-bug your system

If you work on a computer, you probably save your valuable, creative files, delete all the rubbish and check for bugs. Our brains are the most sophisticated computers we'll ever own, but we don't look after them as well as we look after our PCs. However, did you know you can programme your brain to boost your self-esteem?

> **Congratulate yourself when things go right – even little things like getting to work on time or remembering to call a friend on their birthday**

- Use the right programming language and be positive when you talk to yourself. Instead of saying 'I shouldn't eat so much', 'I mustn't be so lazy', 'I can't cope under pressure', use phrases such as 'I can eat healthy food', 'I will take regular exercise', 'I am getting more confident'.

iVillage.co.uk

- Congratulate yourself when things go right – even little things like getting to work on time or remembering to call a friend on their birthday.
- If something is bothering you, whether it's a person, an incident, or something you did or didn't do, acknowledge it, learn from it and then delete it. It's taking up valuable mind space and undermining your self-esteem.
- Before you go to sleep, think of six things that made you happy during the day. It could be a smile, a piece of music, sunshine on your back or a cuddle.
- Use your sleeping time positively. If something's bothering you, ask yourself some questions about it before you go to sleep. Make sure you phrase those questions positively – don't ask yourself 'why am I such a failure?' before you close your eyes. Ask 'how can I be more successful/confident/ happy?'

2. Start the day right

Mornings seem to be a bad time for most people, and if you start off sluggishly, this negative mood can hang around until lunchtime. Put yourself in a positive frame of mind before you even get out of bed by asking yourself these questions:

- If I went to sleep last night with a question in mind, am I any closer to an answer now? (If you don't have that answer yet, don't chase it. Wait until it comes.)
- What am I happy about in my life? (It doesn't have to be large or wonderful. Small happinesses count.)
- What am I excited about?
- What am I proud of?
- What am I grateful for?
- What am I committed to?
- Who do I love?
- Who loves me?

3. Cultivate your social life

People with high self-esteem are generally quite sociable. But this is a chicken-and-egg situation – the less you interact with other people, the more negative you'll feel about yourself and the less likely you'll be to put yourself in social situations.

Break the negative circle by starting to include other people in your life. If this seems difficult, think of it as giving as well as taking. Join a voluntary organisation or club and offer to help. This is not only a distraction from your problems, but also generates feelings of self-worth.

4. Get some exercise

Include more exercise in your life. Working out, particularly outdoors, is a great way to generate your own 'feel-good' chemicals and will give you body confidence as well as energise you. People who exercise regularly tend to look good, they have better skin tone, better muscle tone and their movements are easier and more balanced. If you have physical poise and strength, it's much easier to feel confident inside as well.

5. Relax

Do you spend a lot of time feeling anxious and stressed? Learning to breathe like a relaxed and confident person will help you cope with daily stresses, and it's the simplest habit you could ever learn.

Start treating yourself the way you'd treat your best friend. It comes as a shock to most people how nasty and neglectful we can be to ourselves

---

There are lots of books and classes about this and, if you like the idea, you could take up meditation or yoga and become a master of poise and positive energy.

6. Make your own choices

Take time out to assess a) your career and b) your relationships. Ask yourself:

- Is this job/person giving me positive feedback?
- Do I enjoy this job/person?
- Does this job/person acknowledge and reflect my creativity and my strengths?
- Am I sticking with this job/person simply out of habit?
- Could I do better?

If it's not working for you, whatever it is, change it.

7. Review your situation

Include time for reflection in your daily schedule – praying if you're religious, meditating or writing a diary of your thoughts and feelings. We often don't give ourselves enough time to process all the things that are going on in our lives.

If you decide on a diary, instead of writing a list of what went wrong today, write down these headings first, and fill them in.

- Goals: set yourself a daily outcome and build up to larger goals.
- Achievements: what did you achieve today?
- Gifts: what happened, out of the blue, to cheer you?
- Insights: you may not get one every day – but when you suddenly spot a key to some piece of your behaviour, write it down.

8. Change your environment

Chances are, your environment reflects the way you feel, but, whether it's dull, cluttered or messy, you can change it. Any positive changes you make are going to have a positive effect on your mood too. Look at your desk, your home or even your wardrobe and see what you can do to make it more inspiring.

- Clear up the clutter (a good Feng Shui practice that will make you feel more energetic) and throw out stuff you don't use.
- Give yourself a sound track – add some inspiring music.
- Introduce new bold colours that you love.

9. Give yourself the VIP treatment

Start treating yourself the way you'd treat your best friend. It comes as a shock to most people how nasty and neglectful we can be to ourselves. If you aren't sure you can keep this up for long, take it a day at a time. Give yourself encouragement and support. Take yourself out for a hairdo, a massage, an aromatherapy session – or even a clothes-shopping trip.

10. Find a role model

If you're having difficulty taking this new version of yourself seriously, why not pretend to be someone else? Think of someone you admire – it could be someone you know, or someone famous – and live your day as they would. How would they react to others? Would they be assertive? Relaxed? Confident? Fun and energetic?

And yes, you do know how to do this. Even if you have to think back to when you were a child, you'll be able to come up with a time when you were happy with yourself and in control of your situation. In fact, if you can remember that time very well, why not be your own role model?

Judith Verity is also a slimming coach and author of Quick Fix Your Life *(How To Books, £5.95). Contact the Lighten Up slimming programme on 020 8241 2323 or look at Lightenup.co.uk.*

- Information from iVillage. Visit www.ivillage.co.uk for more information.

© iVillage

Nature has ways of making us feel better

Walking, riding, fishing – or just looking at the countryside – can boost people's self-esteem, according to new research. Thea Jourdan reports

Helena Singleton leans to stroke Nobby the sheep and takes a deep breath of country air. She smiles with pleasure as she buries her hands in the ram's thick fleece. Helena, a typical teenager in hipster jeans and a trendy parka, lives in a built-up area of Blackpool. She has never been this close to a live sheep before.

> *There is increasing evidence to show that getting close to nature can make us feel less stressed and better about ourselves*

The air at Haydock Park race-course in Newton-le-Willows is bracing, but refreshingly clear of pollution. Helena, 14, is one of 1,500 Merseyside schoolchildren taking part in Countryside Live, a children's country fair sponsored by the Countryside Agency, which is dedicated to bringing the countryside to pupils of inner-city schools. As well as meeting rare sheep breeds, gun dogs, wild birds and ferrets, the children are encouraged to try angling, willow weaving and cheese-making. Interactive workshops show them how to enjoy a healthier lifestyle in the great outdoors.

Helena, who is a pupil at Highfield Humanities College in Blackpool, is enjoying her unusual day out. 'Being out in the country is really calming,' she says, gazing out over the green paddocks. 'Just looking at a beautiful scene makes me feel better.'

There is increasing evidence to show that getting close to nature can make us feel less stressed and better about ourselves. A new study, from the University of Essex, shows that 'green' exercise can boost mood, physical fitness and self-esteem.

Professor Jules Pretty, who led the research team at the department of biological science, measured the mood and self-esteem of 263 people who took part in 10 different 'green' activities, such as walking, mountain biking and canal boating.

'We found that there was a significant improvement in self-esteem in nine out of 10 case studies,' says Prof Pretty. 'The majority of people also found that, after participating in the activity, their anxiety levels dropped. They felt less depressed and more upbeat.'

In biochemical terms, the participants experienced enhanced moods because hormones such as oxytocin and endorphins were circulating around their bodies. 'Levels of these hormones went up, which activated the pleasure centre in the brain,' explains Prof Pretty. 'This led to a deep feeling of wellbeing and relaxation.'

Interestingly, angling is one of the best ways to enjoy the feel-good factor of the natural world. The sport, which boasts an impressive following of 3.8 million people in Britain, tops the study's list for boosting self-esteem and mood. This does not surprise Martin James, a registered coach at the National Federation of Anglers: 'Fishing is a kind of therapy. It's also a great way to reduce stress.

'When you fish, you are concentrating on the rod and the water, and everything else is forgotten.'

Essex University's research also found that, when measuring the impact of green activities on mental wellbeing, their duration was not significant. 'A half-hour walk gave the same benefit as a six-hour fishing trip,' says Prof Pretty, who has made another interesting discovery: even gazing at an image of the countryside is good for your health.

Tests conducted on 100 healthy volunteers who ran on treadmills showed that looking at a pleasant rural view caused blood pressure to fall. Conversely, looking at an

unpleasant urban environment had a huge impact: blood pressure rose by an average of eight points. 'This is hugely significant,' says Prof Pretty. 'A view from a window, or even a static image, makes a difference to your wellbeing.'

The findings are supported by a study at Johns Hopkins University, Baltimore in America. Doctors focused on two groups of patients who were in hospital, awaiting operations.

While they listened to piped sounds of birds and running water, one group was shown an image of a beautiful landscape. The other group, however, was left in a room with no view and no sound. Following their operations, the former required significantly less pain control and left hospital sooner than the latter.

'In reality, it must be better for you to smell and touch the real thing, but a good approximation is still helpful,' says Prof Pretty.

At Crompton House School, in Oldham, teachers have decided to bring nature into the classroom.

'I am convinced that nature is good for health,' says teacher Dave Leggett. 'I can see the effect it has on the children when they get into the countryside and the clean air. Immediately, they become more relaxed and more alert. For this reason, we actively encourage pupils to get closer to nature. The lack of green space does not have to be a barrier.'

Pupils are encouraged to join the thriving nature club Roots and Shoots, which aims to preserve wildlife. The school also hopes to build a wildlife garden, where there will be a bog area and viewing benches. Jodie Flint, 11, says: 'I can't wait to see the bog. I just hope there will be lots of dragonflies and frogs.'

Penny Jones, senior advisor at the Countryside Agency, hopes that a new generation of schoolchildren will learn to connect with the natural world.

'We have to look to the future,' she says. 'The Essex University study adds weight to what people have always known: contact with nature and the countryside improves your health.'

■ For further information, see www.countrysidelive.org.uk.

21 March 2005

© Telegraph Group Limited, London 2006

Building self-esteem

You're a winner. You really are. Here's how to bring out the champ from the chump

Get motivated

Everyone can find the confidence to feel better about themselves, but you have to want to do it. Even if you kick off with a minor achievement, like holding your own in a conversation, it'll feed the courage of your convictions.

Find a starting point

No matter how low your self-opinion, identify one thing about yourself that other people like and admire. It doesn't have to be much, from your sense of humour to your kindness among friends, and then build on it. Simple as that!

Stay positive

Don't be down on yourself when people show an interest in you. Instead of being 'not great' or 'could be better' if someone asks how you're doing, why not try being 'fine', or 'really well'? Give it a go, and you'll quickly pick up on the improvement in their response to you.

Be nice

Sometimes when people feel insecure they try to deflect attention away from themselves by being critical of others. Sadly, it says more about them than the poor souls they're bitching about. If this rings a bell with you, then next time try paying compliments. Being nice about someone means others will think better of you, which can only improve the way you see yourself.

Learn from mistakes

If you don't think much of yourself it's easy to be your own worst critic. Things can get worse when others have a go at you, which is why it's so important to take criticism positively. If you screw up, or someone accuses you of making a mess of things, ask if there's anything you can take on board from the episode. See it as a learning experience, not another reason to feel lousier.

Assert yourself

In sticky situations, people with low self-esteem often compensate by being aggressive. The trouble is it tends to alienate people, reinforcing their own view that they don't match up to the rest of humanity. The way forward is by being assertive instead of aggressive. So don't get angry next time you feel as if your opinions are being ignored. Just politely argue your case. The calmer you remain, the more likely it is that your voice will be heard, and the better you'll feel in the long run!

■ The above information is reprinted with kind permission from TheSite.org. Visit www.thesite.org for more information.

© TheSite.org

■ There are any number of apparently confident people who can do marvellous things but who have poor self-esteem. Many people in the public eye fall into this category. (page 1)

■ The word 'esteem' comes from a Latin word which means 'to estimate'. So, self-esteem is how you estimate yourself. (page 1)

■ One of the areas that people with low self-esteem have greatest difficulty with is criticism – giving as well as receiving it. (page 2)

■ People with low self-esteem believe that any successes they achieve are attributable to luck rather than ability or competence. Equally, anything negative can be put down to factors beyond their control. (page 4)

■ Bullies and many criminals are much more likely to suffer from unrealistically high self-esteem and impulse control problems than low self-esteem. (page 7)

■ The overexposure to the media directs young people to examine their bodies and even measure their physical appearance against unrealistic computer-enhanced images. (page 10)

■ A survey of 500 school pupils by the Young Women's Christian Association revealed that one in three thought about their body shape all the time and only 14% were happy with the way they look. (page 12)

■ Although it is more often women and girls who worry about being overweight, national statistics show that in fact only 33% of women are classed as 'overweight', compared with 47% of men. (page 12)

■ The body fat of models and actresses portrayed in the media is at least 10% less than that of healthy women. (page 13)

■ Women who are asked to point to pictures that most closely resemble the shape and size of their body routinely pick women who are larger than themselves. (page 14)

■ White, heterosexual women in the higher social classes, living in westernised countries are most dissatisfied with their size and shape. (page 14)

■ The ideal shape tends to be whatever is most difficult to achieve during a given time period. (page 16)

■ Social factors implicated in the development of eating disorders include sociocultural norms regarding thinness, eating, food preparation and roles of women. (page 17)

■ Few British women are confident about their looks, with just one in five considering themselves attractive. (page 19)

■ Just 8% of teenage girls in Britain deem themselves to be happy with their body, according to a body image survey commissioned by a teen magazine. A further 68% believe their faces to be unattractive, and their lives are preoccupied by the desire to acquire a 'perfect' celebrity body. (page 20)

■ Six out of ten Brits (57 per cent) believe that plastic surgery is the key to true happiness. (page 21)

■ A survey of 2,000 teenage boys, whose average age was 15, found that they are as self-conscious about their bodies as girls, with 62 per cent not liking their faces and 68 per cent not liking their teeth. (page 23)

■ Women had 89% of all cosmetic procedures in 2005 (19,601, up from 15,019 in 2004). (page 24)

■ Almost half (46.9 per cent) of 81 five- to eight-year-olds surveyed wanted to be thinner, and 45.7 per cent said they would go on a diet if they gained weight. (page 25)

■ By the time they reach adulthood, 95 per cent of women are dissatisfied with their bodies and seven out of 10 girls have been on a diet. (page 25)

■ A British study showed that Asian-British women were more content with their body size than White British women, despite the fact that the Asians' ideal body size was as slim as that of the White women. (page 29)

■ Our self-esteem is bound up with our physical wellbeing, and is vulnerable to illness and injury. (page 31)

■ Children tend not to have much power or status in our society, and therefore may still be subject to many common experiences that can undermine their self-esteem. These include, in particular, violence, loss and neglect. (page 32)

■ If you are feeling low, anxious or lacking in confidence, the first thing to do is to stop thinking and relax properly. (page 35)

■ There is increasing evidence to show that getting close to nature can make us feel less stressed and better about ourselves. A new study, from the University of Essex, shows that 'green' exercise can boost mood, physical fitness and self-esteem. (page 38)

■ In sticky situations, people with low self-esteem often compensate by being aggressive. (page 39)

GLOSSARY

Affirmations
Positive statements which may be used by someone suffering from low self-esteem to help change their attitude: for example, 'I am a determined individual capable of achieveing my goals.'

Assertiveness
The ability to demonstrate confidence and forcefulness.

The 'Beauty Myth'
The idea that there is only one form of beauty which we should all aim to achieve.

Blepharoplasty
Cosmetic surgery which changes the appearance of the eyelids. This was the second most popular cosmetic procedure in 2005.

Body image
The mental picture we form of our own body: its shape, size and attractiveness. Whether this image is realistic or not (for example, if we see ourselves as overweight when we are not) can depend upon ideas of the 'perfect body' put forward by society and the media.

Cosmetic surgery
Also called plastic surgery. A medical procedure carried out to change the way a person looks. Current trends suggest that more people are having non-essential cosmetic surgery to correct what they see as problems with their bodies.

Eating disorders
Self-inflicted dietary ilnesses that are linked to extreme poor body image include bulimia and anorexia nervosa.

Liposcution
A form of cosmetic surgery which extracts excess fat from under the skin.

The media
These include film and television programmes, newspapers and magazines, and advertisements on posters and billboards. The media are often blamed for maintaining impossibly high standards of beauty by featuring (often computer-enhanced) images of thin celebrities, causing body dissatisfaction in ordinary people who find this standard impossible to achieve.

Otoplasty
Cosmetic surgery which changes the appearance of the ears. 1,176 people had this treatment in 2005.

Rhinoplasty
Cosmetic surgery which changes the appearance of the nose. This was the most popular cosmetic operation for men in 2005.

Self-esteem
The ability to value and respect ourselves as individuals, and to appreciate our own abilities. Self-belief, self-confidence and self-respect are all attributes of self-esteem.

Self-judgement
The process of measuring ourselves against a standard we have created, often based on what we see as the expectations of others.

Tagging
When someone 'tags', or labels, themselves in a negative way on the basis of one misjudgement or error, for example, someone who labels themselves a 'bad person' based on one mistake.

INDEX

over-generalisation and low self-esteem 6

physical health and self-esteem 31, 33
plastic surgery *see* cosmetic surgery
positive body image 10
positive thinking 2, 6
power and self-esteem 4, 31-2
praise 34
prejudice in childhood, and low self-esteem 32
psychological health, requirements for 8

reflection and self-esteem 37
relaxation and self-esteem 35, 37
rhinoplasty 27
role models
    boys 23
    and self-esteem 37
rural views and mental well-being 38-9

saying no 3
school nature studies 39
self-blame 6
self-criticism 6, 34
self-esteem 1-9
    and body image 10-11
    contributory factors 4, 31-3
    definition 1, 31
    and green activities 38-9
    healthy 30

improving 1-2, 6, 33-9
    questionnaire 9
    see also high self-esteem; low self-esteem
self-image *see* body image
self-judgement 4
singing, and building self-esteem 33
social interaction and low self-esteem 4
social life and self-esteem 36
stress reduction and self-esteem 33
style icons, boys 23
success, attitude to 8

tagging and low self-esteem 6
teenage girls
    body image 20-21
    eating habits 20
    and plastic surgery 26-8
television and body image 11-12
    children 22
thoughts
    and healthy self-esteem 30
    and low self-esteem 5, 6
treats and self-esteem 37

Western society and female body image 16-17
women, body image 19
    and ethnicity 29-30
    and media pressure 11-12, 14-15
    timeline 16-17

ADDITIONAL RESOURCES

Other Issues titles
If you are interested in researching further the issues raised in *Self-Esteem and Body Image*, you may want to read the following titles in the **Issues** series as they contain additional relevant articles:

- Vol. 68 *Coping with Depression* (ISBN 1 86168 250 6)

- Vol. 69 *The Media* (ISBN 1 86168 251 4)

- Vol. 70 *Adolescent Health* (ISBN 1 86168 252 2)

- Vol. 72 *Obesity and Eating Disorders* (ISBN 1 86168 254 9)

- Vol. 73 *Dealing with Bullies* (ISBN 1 86168 255 7)

- Vol. 77 *Self-Inflicted Violence* (ISBN 1 86168 266 2)

- Vol. 84 *Mental Wellbeing* (ISBN 1 86168 279 4)

- Vol. 88 *Food and Nutrition* (ISBN 1 86168 289 1)

- Vol. 100 *Stress and Anxiety* (ISBN 1 86168 314 6)

- Vol. 108 *Domestic Violence* (ISBN 1 86168 328 6)

- Vol. 112 *Women, Men and Equality* (ISBN 1 86168 345 6)

- Vol. 113 *Fitness and Health* (ISBN 1 86168 346 4)

For more information about these titles, visit our website at www.independence.co.uk/publicationslist

Useful organisations
You may find the websites of the following organisations useful for further research:

- The British Association of Aesthetic Plastic Surgeons: www.baaps.org.uk

- British Medical Association: www.bma.org.uk

- Dove Self-Esteem Fund: www.campaignforrealbeauty.co.uk

- The Eating Disorders Association: www.edauk.com

- The F-Word: www.thefword.org.uk

- GetEsteem.com: www.getesteem.com

- The LaBelle Foundation: www.selfesteem.org

- Mind: www.mind.org.uk

- Shining Bright: www.shining-bright.co.uk

- The Site: www.thesite.org

- Uncommon Knowledge: www.self-confidence.co.uk

ACKNOWLEDGEMENTS

The publisher is grateful for permission to reproduce the following material.

While every care has been taken to trace and acknowledge copyright, the publisher tenders its apology for any accidental infringement or where copyright has proved untraceable. The publisher would be pleased to come to a suitable arrangement in any such case with the rightful owner.

Chapter One: Self-Esteem – The Facts

Self-esteem, © NetDoctor, *Background to self-esteem and how it can evolve*, © Shining Bright, *What is low self-esteem?*, © Shining Bright, *Is high self-esteem a bad thing?*, © Uncommon Knowledge Ltd, *Mistaken ways of thinking*, © Eating Disorders Association, *Top ten facts about low self-esteem*, © Uncommon Knowledge Ltd, *Self-esteem questionnaire*, © Marilyn J. Sorensen.

Chapter Two: Self-Esteem and Body Image

Body image and self-esteem, © Soul Food, *Body image*, © The F-Word, *The Dove Self-Esteem Fund*, © Unilever, *How can we learn to love our bodies?*, © Channel 4, *Female body image timeline*, © TheSite.org, *Eating disorders, body image and the media*, © British Medical Association, *Do you have body angst?*, © iVillage, *We hate our bodies*, © 2006 Associated Newspaper Ltd, *Celebrities distort girls' search for ideal shape*, © Guardian Newspapers Ltd 2005, *Plastic fantastic*, © Lloyds TSB, *'My daughter wants surgery . . . she is 13'*, © Telegraph Group Ltd 2005, *Boys and body image*, © Telegraph Group Ltd 2005, *Over 22,000 surgical procedures in 2005*, © BAAPS, *Children's body image*, © Telegraph Group Ltd 2005, *Little miss perfect*, © Telegraph Group Ltd 2006, *Ethnicity and body image*, © TheSite.org, *Healthy self-esteem*, © Shining Bright.

Chapter Three: Raising self-esteem

How to increase your self-esteem, © Mind, *Kick the habit of self-criticism*, © iVillage, *7 ways to boost your self-esteem quickly*, © Uncommon Knowledge Ltd, *Ten ways to boost your self-esteem*, © iVillage, *Nature has ways of making us feel better*, © Telegraph Group Ltd 2006, *Building self-esteem*, © TheSite.org.

Photographs and illustrations:

Pages 1, 16, 28, 38: Don Hatcher; pages 2, 24, 37: Angelo Madrid; pages 8, 20, 34: Simon Kneebone; pages 10, 23: Pumpkin House; pages 13, 26: Bev Aisbett.

Craig Donnellan
Cambridge
April, 2006